DREAMS
WHAT THEY MEAN

Find out what dreams can say about your
hopes, fears and everyday experiences

RICHARD CRAZE

southwater

This edition is published by Southwater

Southwater is an imprint of Anness Publishing Ltd
Hermes House, 88–89 Blackfriars Road
London SE1 8HA
tel. 020 7401 2077; fax 020 7633 9499
www.southwaterbooks.com; info@anness.com

© Anness Publishing Ltd 2004

UK agent: The Manning Partnership Ltd
6 The Old Dairy, Melcombe Road, Bath BA2 3LR
tel. 01225 478444; fax 01225 478440
sales@manning-partnership.co.uk

UK distributor: Grantham Book Services Ltd
Isaac Newton Way, Alma Park Industrial Estate,
Grantham, Lincs NG31 9SD
tel. 01476 541080; fax 01476 541061
orders@gbs.tbs-ltd.co.uk

North American agent/distributor:
National Book Network
4501 Forbes Boulevard, Suite 200, Lanham, MD 20706
tel. 301 459 3366; fax 301 429 5746
www.nbnbooks.com

Australian agent/distributor: Pan Macmillan Australia
Level 18, St Martins Tower, 31 Market St,
Sydney, NSW 2000
tel. 1300 135 113; fax 1300 135 103
customer.service@macmillan.com.au

New Zealand agent/distributor: David Bateman Ltd
30 Tarndale Grove, Off Bush Road, Albany, Auckland
tel. (09) 415 7664; fax (09) 415 8892

A CIP catalogue record for this book is available
from the British Library.

PUBLISHER: Joanna Lorenz
SENIOR EDITOR: Joanne Rippin
EDITOR: Elizabeth Woodland
ADDITIONAL TEXT: Raje Airey and Jenny Barrett
PICTURE RESEARCHER: Frances Vargo
For picture acknowledgements see p160
DESIGNER: Adelle Morris
JACKET DESIGNER: Elizabeth Healey
PRODUCTION CONTROLLER: Darren Price

Previously published as part of a larger volume,
Dream Dictionary

1 3 5 7 9 10 8 6 4 2

CONTENTS

INTRODUCTION

Every dream has one or more major themes or individual elements that seem to hold particular significance in the context of that dream. Often there will be several themes running concurrently, or a handful of elements or qualities that seem important, and each should be investigated and seen in relation to the others.

So for instance, if you dreamt about being chased across a mountain top by a dark man on a wet night, some themes you can look up would be pursuit, mountain, man, stranger, darkness, night, rain, danger, and whatever emotions you felt in the dream. Because there are several elements working together in this example, a dream like this may take quite a lot of work to understand fully, or it may all fall into place quite simply if the dream points up major issues in your life that you are struggling with or if the symbols have strong, clear meanings to you.

ASSOCIATIONS

It is useful to start by noting whether any of the themes or elements have any obvious personal associations or connotations. Often these may have been formed by significant events or situations in your past, but sometimes they may be somewhat random – for instance if the lyrics in some music you were

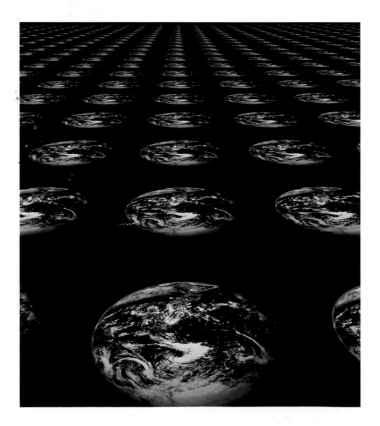

listening to before you went to bed made you think of someone you know or sparked off a memory of some period in your life.

If you have any pressing preoccupations or are undergoing important changes in your life – such as moving house or beginning a new job – you can use these as your starting point and see if the symbolism or story in your dream seems pertinent.

CONTEXT

The significance of something that appears in a dream can be quite varied, even contradictory, and the conventional dream dictionary approach does not take into account personal meanings, or the fact that the context of the dream elements and the relationship between them is essential to the meaning of each element and the dream as a whole.

For example, in its basic interpretation a feast may signify wealth and abundance to you, but whether you are the host, a guest at a king's banquet, or serving others, whether the food and wine are unlimited or in short supply, and whether the food is delicious or inedible, normal or bizarre, all provide essential information regarding how you feel about wealth and abundance, and how they are relevant in your life. It is much more effective and rewarding to try to understand the dream from your own point of view rather than have meanings assigned without any reference to the dream or the dreamer. This book suggests meanings for many elements that you may encounter in your dreams, but you are encouraged to work with these creatively to generate your own understanding of your dreams, rather than accept them as simple truths with only one interpretation.

FRAGMENTS

Not all parts of the dream will be accessible to you – some symbolism may remain hidden, or you will simply forget parts of the dream. If these memories don't return, you may be trying to see the big picture when half of it is missing. You may well remember enough of the dream to get the gist of it and work out its meaning, but what has been lost may have been the greater part, the importance of the dream, and what you remember of the dream could be a mere snippet, a fragment.

If whatever the dream was trying to draw your attention to is lost in this way, you can be sure that your unconscious will try again another time. The images next time round may be similar or quite different, but the meaning or the message will stay the same.

Trust in dreams, for in them is the hidden gate to eternity.   KAHLIL GIBRAN

ABOVE The landscape of your dream is one of the most important aspects of dream analysis.

LEFT Dreams allow you to travel through time and space, and visit realms that only exist inside your imagination.

RIGHT Aspects of the divine can also be a part of your dreams, and can help you to make contact with your subconscious in a profound and remarkable way.

ABOVE Travelling into your own dream world can be one of the most amazing journeys you will ever undertake, and one that you can repeat every night of your life.

LEFT Are dreams tunnels or stairways into other worlds? There are no limits in your dream world, anything and everything is possible.

RIGHT The shapes and textures that appear in your dream can have as profound a message as the characters and feelings, the trick is to remember the detail so that you can analyse the meanings when you wake.

ABSTRACT QUALITIES

The properties of the countless people, objects and ideas that we encounter in our dreams can be highly significant when we are trying to work out what our dreams mean. We may focus on particular qualities because they are so dominant, or because they are distorted or unusual. Abstract concepts such as time and space, power or number, may hold a particular relevance in your dream, either pointing to a literal preoccupation or working symbolically.

When properties that we would take for granted are changed it is almost certainly significant. To work with these elements you need to note what it is that has changed and consider the qualities and meaning of that object as it is in real life as well as how it is in your dream. Occasionally in our dreams abstract concepts are so important that we divest them of all associations, then we can focus on the feelings that such dreams generate.

TIME AND SPACE

ABOVE If you are in a wide open space with far-off horizons in your dreams, is this telling you something about how you feel about your waking life? Do open spaces intimidate you or do you find them stimulating?
ABOVE RIGHT Looking at how we view time and space in our dreams can reveal a lot about how we believe we fit into the universe as a whole.
ABOVE FAR RIGHT Dreaming of the tools of measurement might be an indication that we are sizing ourselves up, working out how we fit in with the things around us.

WE LIVE AS PHYSICAL BEINGS IN A PHYSICAL WORLD AND OUR LIVES UNFOLD OVER TIME. THESE TWO VERY OBVIOUS FACTS PROFOUNDLY AFFECT HOW WE LIVE OUR LIVES — AND THOSE WHO LEAD A MODERN, URBAN LIFESTYLE, WITH ITS CONSTANT ACTIVITY, RUSHING AND LIMITED SPACE, WILL BE ESPECIALLY AWARE OF THEM. DREAMS THAT FEATURE TIME AND SPACE — OUR RELATIONSHIP TO THEM, WHETHER THERE IS TOO MUCH OR TOO LITTLE OF EACH — CAN TELL US MUCH ABOUT THE QUALITY OF OUR LIVES.

SCALE AND DISTANCE

We are affected by the amount of space we have around us and by how near to or how far we are from other people and objects. A small room may feel cosy and intimate or frustratingly restrictive. Cathedrals are built on a massive scale not only to accommodate large congregations but also to represent the power of God and to inspire awe, and perhaps feelings of insignificance.

It can be useful to look at how we feel in relationship to the spaces in which we find ourselves in our dreams, as this can point to how comfortable we are as physical beings, whether we are feeling protected or exposed, and how isolated or crowded out we are feeling. The extreme of this is found in outer space, where we are truly unconstrained by the bounds of our earthly lives or physicality.

POSITION

Where we are in relation to other objects in our dreams may also be worth noting. Being above or in front of something could indicate that we are asserting ourselves in relation to what the object is representing symbolically, feeling self-confident or dominant. Conversely, being below or behind something could point to feelings of inferiority or subser-vience, an urge to hide or be protected — or it could be that we are being invisible or "not seeing" something important.

MEASUREMENT

Rulers, weighing scales and other instruments of measurement show a particular focus on size, distance, scale or space — how near or far, how tall or long or short something is. We are

NEVER-ENDING DREAM

"In my dream I was ironing. Each article seemed to take as long to iron as it would have in real life. I remember thinking – or dreaming – about how boring this was, how boring my life was, how boring everything was.

When I woke up after what seemed to be hours of ironing I was almost screaming with boredom. I realized that my life was really tedious and I worried that I was a bore. I felt that I had to do something about it, and changed a lot after that."

subconsciously measuring ourselves against the world we live in, especially in relation to social expectations. It may also be that we are trying to establish some kind of control over our environments, or using objective means to measure ourselves.

Dreaming of clocks may indicate a preoccupation with time, how it is regulating our lives, perhaps preventing us from having enough time to do the things we want, or having too much time on our hands. In a broader sense timepieces may be reminding us of our mortality.

ELASTICITY OF TIME AND SPACE

Time in dreams is very flexible, becoming distorted, elongated or slowed down. First there is the fact that dreams that seem to last an age might have occurred in only a second. Within the dream itself, distortions of time may relate to feeling out of control – perhaps everything is happening faster than you can cope with, or you are trying to get somewhere fast but don't seem to be moving.

As time can be stretched out or compressed in our dreams, so too can space. In a flash we can travel from one end of the universe to another, between worlds, between states of consciousness. Space can become condensed and compressed, or we become expanded, to such an extent that we can actually fill the universe. In such cosmic dreams we address our beliefs in the

nature of the universe, and how we feel about our place within it.

In a dream your attention may be drawn to a preoccupation with space or time by the fact that it is distorted. *Alice in Wonderland* is a story about a dream in which the bewildered and frustrated heroine finds herself too big or small for what she wants to do or for the space in which she finds herself.

ABOVE Crowded areas full of people and activity might give you a feeling of unease, or even terror, or you might find them the most reassuring and natural places to be.
ABOVE LEFT Cosmic dreams about how planet Earth is positioned might be a way of establishing your own position in your personal universe.
ABOVE FAR LEFT Do you feel that time is slipping away from you in your waking life? Perhaps this feeling will be reflected in your dreams.
LEFT In our dreams, the boundaries between time and space can become blurred and we discover new dimensions. In dream time vast epics are played out in what seems an age but is, in real time, only seconds.

SCIENCE AND NUMBERS

SOMETIMES THE UNIVERSE APPEARS ORDERLY AND RATIONAL, AND AT OTHER TIMES IT SEEMS RANDOM AND CHAOTIC. IN DREAMS OF SCIENCE OR ONES IN WHICH NUMBERS SEEM PARTICULARLY SIGNIFICANT, WE ARE TRYING TO RESOLVE THESE CONTRADICTIONS AND MAKE SENSE OF THE WORLD AROUND US; WE WANT TO IMPOSE OUR OWN SENSE OF RATIONALITY AND CONTROL OVER OUR LIVES. SCIENCE GIVES US A MEASURE OF CONTROL OVER THE UNIVERSE AND STOPS US FEELING QUITE SO SMALL OR POWERLESS. TOGETHER WITH NUMBERS IT PUTS US ON A PAR WITH THE GODS, AND CAN GIVE US A FEELING OF CONTROL AND POWERFULNESS, WHICH CAN BE REFLECTED IN OUR DREAMS.

A SCIENTIFIC APPROACH

The discipline and rationality of science makes it a strongly intellectual activity, as we push back the boundaries of knowledge with little regard for emotional or intuitive responses. Because science is much esteemed in our society, we may seek shelter behind its authority to avoid facing our emotions or dealing with irrationality. On the other hand, the strict scientific approach to understanding may seem unnecessarily restrictive to more expressive people.

In dreams that involve science it might well also be that we are abdicating responsibility for working out what makes the universe tick. We may not believe in a divine force so we hold fast to the idea that science will work it out for us.

CALCULATIONS

Numbers provide a way of quantifying aspects of our world, and we may dream of them to give us a sense of control, rationality and certainty if these are lacking in our lives. We use them in calculations, so working with figures may indicate that you are trying to take a methodical and "calculating" approach to a situation, rather than following your heart or your intuition.

NUMBERS AS SYMBOLS

Some numbers also have specific symbolic values based on cultural associations. We internalize these values and associations to some extent and may employ them in our dreams. The idea that numbers have mysterious powers has been explored in cultures around the world for millennia. In the West, numerology, as this theory is called, not only assigns particular numbers meanings but also associates them with colours and sound frequencies. If you are familiar with numerology, then such associations may reinforce the significance of the numbers, but you need to establish whether this feels true for you. Some of the values of the numbers in numerology have found their way into our cultural symbolic vocabulary and will probably seem obvious, such as One representing individualism or Two partnership, though others may not resonate particularly strongly for you.

Like all dream elements, numbers can have a personal significance as well as, in some cases, having gained symbolic value in the context of particular cultures. So for a devout Christian, Three could suggest the Holy Trinity; a musician may see it as the foundation chord of the scale, while for another

BELOW As children we play games with numbers. They are a part of our life from early on.
BELOW RIGHT Like all dream subjects, numbers have a personal aspect – what they signify can only mean something to us individually.

LEFT If we don't understand scientific principles, our dream symbols may present science in a negative, perhaps even intimidating, light. **MIDDLE LEFT** Doctors are part of the terrifying science dream symbolism and can appear or be used as distorted dream codes. **BOTTOM LEFT** We may use low-tech imagery such as cogs to represent time and science in our dreams.

person it may bring up the concept of the family trio of father, mother and child. Children often have strong emotional relationships to certain numbers, such as lucky Seven; a triple Six in the Christian tradition is the number of the Devil, while Thirteen has, over the centuries, come to represent bad luck so strongly that even in our modern, rational society there are streets with no house of that number. Even if you are not superstitious, the fact that these associations exist in our society is often borrowed by our mind to suggest something to us. If you relate to a given meaning on a deep and instinctive level then it is significant to you.

NUMEROLOGY

The study of the symbolic value of numbers provides a way of understanding life by studying and exploring their esoteric significance as symbols of the energy of the universe. Numerology readings use numbers that are derived from your birth date and from the letters of your name, these numbers then provide understanding of personal traits that affect how you approach life. Sometimes the system of numerology is used for prophecy.

NUMBER POWER

These are some of the basic characteristics that are assigned to each of the numbers One to Nine in numerology:

1 unity, creation, independence, assertiveness, the self

2 duality, emergence, compromise, discourse

3 power, generative force, creative self-expression

4 solidity, dullness, persistence, determination

5 sensuality, pleasure, gregariousness

6 perfection, harmony, balance, domesticity

7 mysticism, psychic powers, magic

8 materialism, success, justice, ambition

9 spirituality, mental achievement, wisdom

SIGNS AND SYMBOLS

FREUD WROTE AT LENGTH ABOUT SEXUAL SYMBOLS, OF THE MULTITUDE OF OBJECTS IN OUR ORDINARY ENVIRONMENT THAT COULD BE USED TO REPRESENT OR ATTRACT OUR ATTENTION TO SEXUALITY. JUNG EXPLORED SYMBOLIC ARCHETYPES, SUCH AS THE MASK, THE MAGICAL JOURNEY OR THE RITUAL BAPTISM, IN WHICH A PERSON, PLACE OR EVENT COMES TO REPRESENT A SHARED HUMAN EXPERIENCE. IN A SENSE, EVERYTHING DISCUSSED IN THIS BOOK FUNCTIONS AS A SYMBOL IN THE CONTEXT OF OUR DREAMS, BUT WHEN WE TALK ABOUT SIGNS AND CULTURAL OR PERSONAL SYMBOLS WE ARE TALKING ABOUT ACTUAL ICONIC OBJECTS THAT CARRY CERTAIN SIGNIFYING FACTORS.

ABSTRACT QUALITIES

THE COMPLEXITY OF SYMBOLS

In this context, the word "symbols" denotes icons that we use to signify allegiance, power, authority, status, belief systems and so on – such as the cross or swastika or a country's flag. It also covers alphabets and hieroglyphs – symbolic systems that have arisen in cultures around the world to

BELOW In our dreams we will seize on any symbol and put it to virtually any use. Flags, for example, can signify a range of emotions – pride, aggression, power, belonging and alienation, to name a few.

communicate efficiently with others across time and distance.

The difference between these and the other symbols that we discuss in this book is that these have all been generated consciously by people to represent certain things, as a shortcut to communicating a raft of meanings, rather than evolving in a more organic way through human experience. Each of these symbols provides a complexity of meanings, which are reinforced every time we see them, much the same way that corporate or product logos are used to reinforce an image that an organization wants to project.

RELIGIOUS SYMBOLS

Our relationship with religion and spirituality in general, and with particular religions, is addressed by the manifestation of religious symbols in our dreams. These symbols evoke a highly personal response, which depends on our attitude, our own beliefs, any religious experiences we might have had, and so on. The cross, for example, is for many a revered symbol of Christ's love, but it could also be a symbol of suffering (we speak of "having a cross to bear" meaning a burden of responsibility) or even bring to mind the cruelty of religious

persecution and conquest. The Star of David is a common symbol of Judaism, but it may bring associations of oppression and discrimination because of how it was used to mark out Jews in Nazi Germany.

SYMBOLS OF POWER AND AUTHORITY

National flags are associated with particular countries and their assumed or stated cultures and value systems, and so as symbols can be highly emotionally charged – think of how often the flags of certain countries are ceremonially burnt, for instance. In a general sense, they also signify allegiance to a particular country or other political or ideological body, feelings of inclusion and belonging or exclusion, pride or contempt. Flags may also bear particular symbols – the swastika, for instance, is strongly associated with the right-wing ideologies of Nazi Germany, the Holocaust, fascism, regimentation, oppression, pure evil and a host of similar negative associations – although the ancient symbol that the Nazis used as their emblem originally signified the sun, and symbolized good luck.

In an obvious way the crown is a symbol of royalty, but this in itself may mean many things,

LEFT Some symbols, such as the Star of David, are imbued with an almost magical power due to their history.

LEFT Hieroglyphs are a good example of how subjective a language is. Although now an obsolete sign system, they still conjure up certain symbolic significance for us today.

ABOVE In older cultures, everything in nature held a particular meaning and was given symbolic value.

such as authority, inherited power, immense wealth, status and responsibility. A monarch, like a parent, may be either a protective, benevolent authority figure, or a threatening and despotic character who reduces our own freedom. The second kind of monarch embodies an excess of power, wealth and so on, and highlights one's own relative poverty. The scales of justice suggest balance and impartiality, as well as the authority of judges and the legal system in general.

ALPHABETS AND HIEROGLYPHS

We use symbolic systems to communicate – whether they consist of the letters of an alphabet, which represent sounds of speech, the hieroglyphs of ancient Egypt, musical notation or a code such as semaphore.

If we dream of such symbols, whether we understand them or not is crucial. The symbols may be associated with a particular nationality or culture, and understanding them may signify access to that culture, or a denial of that access. Equally, the symbols may indicate that information is being obscured or withheld, or that the dreamer has a lack of clarity, an inability to "read" or "decipher" a situation.

ABOVE Heavenly symbols, such as the sun, the stars and the moon, are a part of the richly symbolic language of religious imagery.
RIGHT Crowns, sceptres and thrones suggest the pomp and majesty of kingship and rule.
BELOW Even something simple and iconic can be given a lofty and weighty symbolism, such as the scales of justice.

CAUSE AND EFFECT

FOR CENTURIES, PHILOSOPHERS, SCIENTISTS AND THEOLOGIANS HAVE GRAPPLED WITH QUESTIONS OF THE ORIGINS OF THE UNIVERSE, AND OF HUMANKIND'S PLACE WITHIN IT. THIS IS THE ULTIMATE QUESTION OF CAUSE AND EFFECT — THE EFFECT IS ALL TOO VISIBLE, BUT THE CAUSE STILL A MATTER OF GREAT DEBATE. ON A MUCH SMALLER SCALE, IN OUR EVERYDAY LIVES, WE ARE FACED WITH CAUSALITY ALL THE TIME — OUR ACTIONS HAVE CONSEQUENCES, WHICH IN TURN HAVE A KNOCK-ON EFFECT, AND WE ARE OFTEN AWARE THAT OUR LIVES HAVE TAKEN A DRAMATIC TURN BECAUSE OF WHAT SEEMED AT THE TIME LIKE AN INSIGNIFICANT OR UNRELATED EVENT.

OUR ORIGINS

Creation myths and theories are part of every human culture. The Big Bang Theory, the Book of Genesis, the Egyptian and classical legends, the Buddhists' Seven Ages of the Universe – all attempt to address the big questions about existence, and all have entirely different starting points and conclusions in looking at the concept of our origins. Some people have a burning need to know how everything came into being and what was behind it. They may use dream time to look for the answers that will enable them to make their own sense of the universe, to formulate and test their belief systems, and to begin to conceptualize the primary force behind our creation. In fact these dreams may be an important way of revealing to us an underlying dissatisfaction with our beliefs, and a dislike of being adrift in uncertainty.

THE RHYTHMS OF THE UNIVERSE

Causation is seen in the constant interplay of the forces of the universe, and all its physical routines – the sun rising and setting, the path of the stars through the night sky, the seasons, nature, beginnings and endings, life and death, birth and growth. Dreams that tackle such fundamental questions as why we are here, where we are going and what we want from life, cause us to sit up and take notice, change direction, even change our lives.

THE FOUR SEASONS

The seasons of the year are a very potent symbol of change and the natural order of things. We use the cycle of spring, summer, autumn and winter as metaphors for the stages of our own life, and we also measure the years by the

BELOW AND BELOW RIGHT How we came into being is a question that has been addressed through human history, from the creation myths of ancient Egypt (below left) to the Islamic prophets of the Middle Ages (below right). We still don't have all the answers, and our dreams will reflect this.

ABOVE Dreams of spring may symbolize new beginnings.
ABOVE RIGHT Summer dreams are often about enjoyment, relaxation, pleasure, warmth and love.

ABOVE Winter dreams may be about closing down, culmination, a decrease of desire and hope, endings and conclusions.
ABOVE LEFT Dreams of autumn may symbolize enrichment, fulfilment, bounty, harvest, and fruitfulness.

turning of the seasons. The significance of nature in our dreams may reflect our feelings of being divorced from nature. Perhaps we live in cities and feel that we are unable to connect with the seasons visually and emotionally, but they still affect us on a very deep level, and if we don't acknowledge this it may surface in our dreams.

EVENTS IN OUR LIVES

We ourselves are agents of change. Everything we say and think and do has an effect on our own lives and on those of others, and sometimes these effects are brought forcefully to our attention. You forget something at home and go back to get it, only to hear on the news that that brief delay meant that you narrowly avoided being involved in a car pile-up. You have a conversation with a friend about your hopes and frustrations with work, and they put you in touch with someone who can make your dream of running your own business a reality.

Awake or asleep, we may turn over in our minds questions of why things happened the way they did, and what might have been if we had done something differently.

Whether you regard these little triggers as chance or fate or part of some greater plan, they all have consequences great and small, and you may turn them over in your mind again and again. If these consequences are negative, you may be plagued by regret or guilt, and these feelings are likely to be played out in dreams by your unconscious mind. You may be trying to work through the events, to find a way to absolve your guilt, to discover that the events were not after all your fault, or wishing that things had happened a different way.

I shall be telling this with a sigh
Somewhere ages and ages hence:
Two roads diverged in a wood, and I –
I took the one less travelled by,
And that has made all the difference.

ROBERT FROST, *THE ROAD NOT TAKEN*

LIFE-CHANGING DREAM

"In my dream I was going to work. I was almost there when the lorry in front of me suddenly slowed to turn, and I sensed that I was going to have an accident. As I powered up the bike and overtook it, I congratulated myself on avoiding a crash. Then another lorry pulled out of a side road and I went straight into it. I could see my motorbike turning over and over in the air in slow motion. I was badly injured.

I was also badly shaken when I woke up, and as a result I gave up that job – I couldn't travel that road any more and my life changed direction completely."

STRENGTH AND WEAKNESS

IN OUR COMPETITIVE WORLD, IT IS NOT SURPRISING THAT DREAMS OF STRENGTH AND WEAKNESS TROUBLE OUR SLEEP AT TIMES. SUCH DREAMS MAY TAKE THE FORM OF CONVENTIONAL SYMBOLISM — THE STRENGTH OF A LION, A WRESTLER, IRON CHAINS OR AN ELECTRIC STORM, OR THE WEAKNESS AND FRAILTY OF A TINY CREATURE, AN OLD OR DISABLED PERSON, A DELICATE SPIDER'S WEB. OR THEY MAY HIGHLIGHT YOUR OWN PERSONAL STRENGTHS AND WEAKNESSES, EITHER LITERAL OR METAPHORIC. WHAT WE THINK OF AS STRENGTH IN OUR WAKING LIFE MAY MANIFEST COMPLETELY DIFFERENTLY IN OUR DREAMS AND WE MAY BE SURPRISED BY OUR OWN SYMBOLISM.

COSMIC STRENGTH

The universe is immense, powerful and strong, and by comparison, we humans are almost absurdly tiny, vulnerable and weak. Cosmic dreams about strength underline the fact of this terrible fragility, as our unconscious tries to come to terms with the size, power, age and complexity of the universe.

We know where we begin and end as individuals, but any similar quantification of the universe is impossible. We know that we will die at some point in time, and that when we do so this immeasurable and intricate universe will continue in all its glory without a second thought.

Our passing and fleeting presence will leave not a trace in any way.

SECURITY

Dreams about strength may be our way of investigating how safe we feel in our waking life. They may be our unconscious mind's way of getting us to do something about feeling insecure. If we live in a dangerous neighbourhood we are likely to have a constant background preoccupation with safety issues and a fear of being threatened unexpectedly; to address this our best course of action could be to learn assertiveness or how to be physically stronger, to build safe zones where we can let down our

guard, or to be more cautious about entering dangerous circumstances or places.

The insecurity that troubles us may be of a more personal nature – in our relationships rather than in the sense of our physical wellbeing – so we should look at why these relationships make us feel that way. Our dream might also be the start of a search for a guardian angel of some kind who will protect us from being overwhelmed by the strength and size of the universe.

WEAKNESS

A dream of strength could be nature's way of drawing our attention to some aspect of our

BELOW LEFT Rather than the obvious images of power or strength, images of gentleness, such as a tiny baby, may be used as a symbol for true strength.
BELOW RIGHT In our dreams, conventional metaphors for strength may appear as clear or distorted images.

defencelessness and vulnerability. If we feel threatened by stronger forces then it makes sense to seek ways of becoming stronger so we are better able to fight off the threat, or of compensating in some other way if this is not possible. The dream is flagging up the fact that we feel weak or frail or naked and we are being urged to do something about that. Where the threat comes from in our waking life is up to us to determine. It might be that we need to find a way of coming to terms with the imponderables of an immense and powerful universe, or it might be more mundane issues, such as our work or our relationships, that are threatening to overwhelm us. Either way, if we feel threatened by strength in a dream then it is likely that there is something that is making us feel threatened or vulnerable in our waking life.

PERSONAL STRENGTHS AND WEAKNESSES

It is probably physical prowess that first springs to mind when you think of strength, but just as important is the personal strength that we draw from being centred and knowing who we are. It may be that we express that centredness symbolically in an image of physical strength. We also describe as strengths and weaknesses the things that we do well or the things that we are not good at. And having a weakness for something means that we like it or are drawn to it so much that we cannot refuse it; although, say, having a weakness for chocolate may seem trivial, it could be a

RIGHT Powerful architectural forms may be used as symbols for strength in our dreams.
MIDDLE RIGHT An awareness of our mental strengths or fragilities may become apparent in our dreams and can cause worry.
BOTTOM RIGHT We may use immense symbols such as the power and strength of the entire universe to bring home a simple truth such as an acknowledgement that we are being used or abused in some way.

signpost to some other area of your life where you lack control. It is worth bearing all possibilities in mind when you are trying to understand your dream, as your mind may be using apparently frivolous concepts as a springboard for exploring more serious issues. How power manifests in our dreams can be a reflection on how secure we feel.

A COSMIC DREAM

"I was alone in the vastness of space but I could feel the sheer size and strength of the universe closing in on me. Everything was black and I couldn't see what forces were pressing against me – it seemed as though it was the very walls of the universe that were crushing me out of existence. I couldn't fight against this sort of strength.

The dream was really quite terrifying, and I woke up feeling small and helpless. It made me realize that I was letting a lot of people walk all over me and needed to be much more assertive, to learn to say 'no' more often, especially at work."

POWER DREAMS

POWER APPEARS IN MANY GUISES — FROM THE OBVIOUS FORMS AND TRAPPINGS OF POLITICAL OR MILITARY POWER AND WEALTH, TO PHYSICAL DOMINATION, OPPRESSION, VICTIMIZATION OR BULLYING, THE AUTHORITY OF AGE OR WISDOM, OR THE PERSONAL POWER OF A TRULY CENTRED INDIVIDUAL. POWER EXERTED OVER US CAN BE A SOURCE OF INSPIRATION, RESPECT, STIMULATION, ENCOURAGEMENT, DEFERENCE AND SAFETY. ON THE OTHER HAND IT CAN PROVOKE FEAR AND HOSTILITY. HOW WE FEEL ABOUT POWER AND INFLUENCE IN REAL LIFE WILL AFFECT HOW WE DREAM OF THEM. DOES POWER EXCITE OR DISMAY YOU? DO YOU FEEL INVIGORATED BY IT OR STIFLED?

Power can manifest itself on a cosmic level – divine, celestial, universal, collective – and also as an attribute of an individual or organization. Dreams in which power is a dominant theme tend to be unambiguous. We are likely to respond strongly to them and to remember them because of this. In them we may be enslaved or motivated; we may even be the source of the power itself.

Our society is highly stratified, and power in a social and political sense is an inevitable part of our lives. Monarchs and presidents wield it over their citizens, bosses over employees, parents over their children. Many people are preoccupied with power, seeking it, being dissatisfied with a lack of it, feeling the effects of the power that others wield. So it is not surprising that images of power crop up in dreams quite often. We may have power thrust upon us, such as when we are promoted to a position of responsibility, and be unsure of how to handle it or of how others will react. We may have bullied

someone and now be feeling guilty. If we pay attention to how power manifests in our dreams and how we respond to it, we may learn about how to deal with the real-life situation that is preoccupying us.

NUCLEAR POWER
We have all grown up in the nuclear age, in which the possibility of being wiped out by nuclear weapons or by an accident at a nuclear power plant has seemed very real. Such power is immense, and used properly, it can enhance the quality of our lives, but if anything goes wrong, and the containment of this power fails or is breached,

BELOW A dream that involves a king figure, or even a godly one may well be a reflection of a feeling you have in your waking life that you are being dominated or controlled in some way.

A DREAM OF GOD

"In my dream, God was sitting on a vast, unearthly throne. But rather than paying attention to being face to face with God, I was fascinated by the throne. Its construction was really important – it was made of some kind of metal, never seen on earth, which was grey flecked with red, and had a luminous transparency like crystal.

I realised that this throne was where the real power lay: whoever sat on it would become a god, and God Himself had only got his power from having been on it for so long. If anyone else sat there, they too would acquire that sort of power. There was no power in the person, only in the throne – the material trappings of power.

I'm not religious at all so I was quite surprised to have had what seemed at first like a religious dream, but I think it was more about knowing where power lies and how to access it than about the spiritual aspect of God. I'm very concerned with power and authority in my life as I am in the police force. My uniform represents these things, but it doesn't make me feel powerful from within; it also creates a negative reaction in some people, which I don't like."

disaster is virtually inevitable. The dreams of many people are affected by such fears, and they need to come to terms with the feeling of helplessness that this kind of threat generates. Because of the "all-or-nothing" feeling that nuclear war has, we may use it to represent in a more general or metaphoric sense the end of the world as we know it, or some personal calamity.

THE POWER OF NATURE

Sometimes nature unleashes its power on a spectacular scale: lightening storms, floods, forest fires, hurricanes and avalanches all put us in our place in the universe. We try to minimize the damage done by these phenomenan, but ultimately we are powerless. An impending natural disaster in a dream – the moment before a dam bursts or a storm breaks – may show us the potential power that we have in ourselves; how we express it may make the difference between greatness and destruction.

COMING TO TERMS WITH POWER

In waking life or in our dreams, we might feel drawn irresistibly to some situation or event or person but cannot understand why. The power that draws us may be invisible and subtle but by careful analysis and observation we might begin to understand what is controlling

us, and can assess what we are being manipulated or influenced by in our waking life.

By paying attention to power dreams we can literally empower ourselves in real life. Once we have pinpointed and understood the powers that we fear, find attractive or wish to develop in ourselves, then they can be tamed and put to use.

ABOVE FAR LEFT When you dream of power is it manifested on an individual basis, with a symbol of social control such as a monarch?
ABOVE LEFT Or does your dream of power involve forces such as those in large-scale industry?
ABOVE Or is it the power that might be unleashed by politicians and rulers that you fear you are unable to control?

LEFT Nature has such awesome power, such highly destructive force, that it may appear in our dreams as a frightening power indeed.

COLOUR

THE MORE AWARE WE ARE OF COLOURS IN OUR LIVES, THE MORE WE ARE LIKELY TO DREAM IN COLOUR. BUT SOMETIMES IN A DREAM, COLOUR DEMANDS OUR ATTENTION, EITHER BECAUSE IT IS VERY STRONG OR BECAUSE IT IS UNNATURAL IN ITS CONTEXT. IN THIS WAY IT ACQUIRES SYMBOLIC VALUE, AND YOU SHOULD CONSIDER WHAT MEANING IT HAS FOR YOU. DO WE ALL DREAM IN COLOUR ALL OF THE TIME? THIS MAY SEEM IRRELEVANT IF YOU ALWAYS DO BUT WHAT IF YOU DREAM IN BLACK AND WHITE? HAVE YOU EVER HAD A DREAM THAT IS IN JUST ONE COLOUR? WHAT DO THE COLOURS WE SEE IN OUR DREAMS MEAN? ARE THEY REFLECTIONS OF OUR EMOTIONS OR OUR SPIRITUALITY?

Some colours we respond to in a very personal way, but many of the associations we have with particular colours are culturally informed – for example, white is worn by the bride on her wedding day in Western culture, but in the Far East it is the colour traditionally worn at funerals.

CREATIVE POWER OF COLOUR

We may be surprised by the intensity of colours in our dream, by the inventiveness of our imagination. But everything in our dream expresses ourselves – what we see is what we are capable of creating. These dreams can awaken in us a sense of our real power, can make us realize how impressive we really are, however much we get bogged down in our day-to-day lives.

EXPRESSING OUR INNER BEING

A dream that focuses on fantastic colour and form – whirling patterns and shifting shapes – may resemble an "acid trip", or it could be that you are making spiritual contact with your inner self. In a rainbow, all the colours are present, and are perfectly, naturally in balance. Strongly contrasting colours may signify either clear choices or a dilemma in some area of your life, while colours that merge and blend could signify an inner harmony, or, conversely, a lack of clarity.

Pay special attention if several dreams feature a particular colour, as this could be your unconscious trying to work with a particular issue that you are not addressing effectively in your waking life. Equally, if you stop focusing on this colour in your dreams then it could be that you have worked through something that was on your mind.

COLOURS BY ASSOCIATION

It is said that the colours we see in our dreams reflect the state of our unconscious mind. So if blue predominates, we may be feeling emotional, while green could suggest an interest in nature or environmental issues. These are only two possible meanings though, and it may be that your mind has randomly drawn on a catchphrase such as "feeling blue" or the Green Party of environmental politics. In the same way, blue has even been suggested as an indicator of futuristic travel because of the phrase "taking off into the blue".

COLOUR KEY

These are some associations people commonly have with particular colours. Remember though that your own personal experiences, as well as cultural differences, may mean that they do not always ring true to you – use them as a starting point to prompt your own feelings, rather than as fact.

Red: energy, fire, passion, love, sex, anger, danger

Orange/yellow: vibrancy, joy, life, sunshine, warmth, spirituality, jealousy

Green: calm, nature, illness, envy

Blue: peace, emotions, depression, space

Violet/purple: grandeur, royalty, rage

White: innocence, energy, emptiness, possibility, cleanliness, holiness

Black: death, mourning, depression, conformity, secrecy, obscurity

ABOVE Nature has her own colour symbolism which may not be for our benefit at all – flowers are coloured for the bees rather than for us.

ABOVE AND ABOVE RIGHT Natural colours, such as shades of green, have instant association with growth and renewal. If you dream of green your subconscious could be sending you a message about decisions that need to be made.

RIGHT Brightly coloured sweets attract children – do the colours have the same impact on you if you dream about them, or do they seem unpleasantly synthetic and confusing?

ABOVE The colour white in Western cultures is synonymous with purity and innocence. Dreaming of white weddings might therefore symbolize this.

LEFT Multicoloured objects in dreams may be a way for your mind to link with your emotions.

BELOW Perhaps there are no symbolic associations with colours in a dream. Vibrant shades might just be a way of your creative mind expressing itself.

The expression "seeing red", meaning to be angry, may well have come from the red mist you see before your eyes if in a severe rage, but it would be simplistic to say that this necessarily means that a dream involving the colour red always points to anger. Our conscious mind might make these easy associations of anger, violence, passion, fire and energy, but the red in your dream could also be the red of romantic love and passion, or a warning of danger. It could even be a "red herring" – perhaps before bed you saw the word "red", or a film in which colour was used for artistic emphasis. Perhaps you told your child the story of Little Red Riding Hood at bedtime. These triggers may lead your mind to cultural meanings that are commonly ascribed to the colour – the dangerous wolf is attracted by the girl's coat; her red coat may have pointed to the danger she was in.

DREAM COLOURS

"I was standing on a hilltop, and could see myself from above, turning round and round in slow motion. I was so aware of the vividness of the grass, the sky, my clothes, everything, and the colours were so bright, that I felt I was being told something. I woke up wanting to paint those colours, although I hadn't picked up a brush for years. I took up painting again because of this dream, and I'm so happy just doing it."

SHAPE, FORM, TEXTURE

LIKE COLOUR, THE SHAPE AND TEXTURE OF OBJECTS AND SPACES CAN HOLD THE KEY TO THE MEANING OF OUR DREAMS. REGULAR GEOMETRIC FORMS CARRY ASSOCIATIONS SIMILAR TO THOSE OF THE NUMBER OF SIDES THEY HAVE, WHILE PROPORTIONS, SUCH AS HOW LONG, TALL OR SHORT, AND HOW FAT OR THIN SOMETHING OR SOMEONE IS, MAY ALSO BE SIGNIFICANT. YOU MAY FOCUS YOUR ATTENTION ON THE TEXTURE OF A SURFACE IN YOUR DREAM, FOCUSING ON WHETHER IT IS SHARP OR BLUNT, SOFT OR SMOOTH, AND ALSO WHETHER IT IS WHOLE OR BROKEN. HOW MUCH DO WE DRAW ON THE SENSE OF TOUCH? DOES EACH SURFACE HAVE TEXTURE?

Many of the above properties may be insignificant in the context of your dream, but if they particularly catch your attention or they are unusual in some way, you can be fairly certain that they are presented like this for a reason. You should ask yourself why it is that a particular shape is appearing in your dream, and if it is markedly different from what you would expect, then look at what the difference is and why your mind has formed the object in this way.

SYMMETRY
Regular shapes have a strong connection with numbers, and because they are so basic and are found in so many aspects of our waking lives – the sides of a geometric form, the number of petals on a flower, how many

points a star has – physical shapes may often be used in dreams metaphorically, to stand in for more abstract or complex concepts.

For example, a circle – whether it is a golden ring or a round room – may suggest harmony, inclusion and femininity, while a square may bring feelings of order and symmetry, masculinity, conventionality or even military precision. A triangular shape to some people may allude to a representation of the perfect balance of the Holy Trinity, the mother-father-child relationship, or the tension of a love triangle. . The pyramid, often thought to have a mystical significance, has a solid base, but in its pinnacle reaches for the sky. Dreaming of this form may show that you are aspiring to greater things.

CURVES AND SPIRALS
Wavy lines are more fluid and often more random than straight lines, and in this may suggest a freedom and unpredictability not found in a more regular form. While straight lines could suggest clarity of vision or thought, twists, loops and curves may indicate obscurity or confusion. Spirals have a strong sense of movement, notice whether they are spiralling inward or outward, and feel whether they are suggestive of something in your life "spiralling out of control" or whether they give you an exhilarating sense of moving outward and upward, away from confinement. By contrast, points and angles may indicate dead ends, especially if viewed from the inside, or show a concentration of energy.

BELOW RIGHT Dreaming of pyramid shapes might have a particular mystical significance for you, or it might be a more prosaic link with your aspirations.
BELOW Dreaming of straight lines, such as a road with no turns or bends, might mean strength of purpose and clarity of vision. It might also mean predictability and lack of self-expression however.

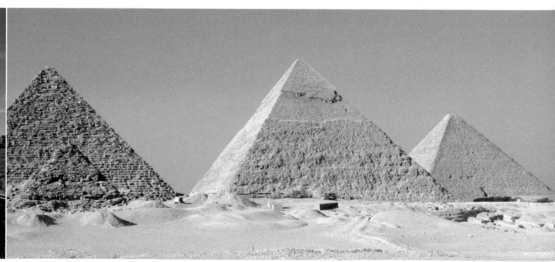

OPEN AND CLOSED FORMS

Whether the form is open or fully enclosed could also be highly significant. A box with its lid off, or an enclosed garden whose gate is open, has nothing to hide, and allows the possibility of moving out of a state of enclosure or confinement whether physical, intellectual or emotional, and of moving on to new experiences.

FAT OR THIN?

Our response to fatness and thinness in people is usually heavily influenced by widely accepted ideals and stereotypes. Your dream may use these stereotypes in a literal way, but you can also look at whether a person's size is associated metaphorically with some attitude to resources. In this way, a fat person – or object or animal – may symbolize plenty and a thin person a lack of resources; alternatively, size may point to a relationship to resources, such as whether you are hoarding or rejecting them, or using them up

faster than you can get hold of them. Fat may also have associations of cuddliness and therefore comfort, or alternatively may indicate lethargy or inaction.

PROPORTIONS

Tall people, buildings and other objects have a physical advantage in their height and can also be seen from a distance. Tall people have stature and can see farther, while from the commanding height of a tall building or hill, one has a greater perspective. Short people, on the other hand, can be looked down on both literally and figuratively, and may have difficulty in having their authority accepted. But smaller

can also mean more nimble or manoeuvrable or can offer the advantage of having an ear close to the ground.

TEXTURE

You may well have an emotional response to the texture of objects in your dream. Sharp edges and rough surfaces may be uncomfortable to the touch, or even threatening. Fuzzy surfaces may be comforting, a reminder of the cuddly toys of childhood, while smooth or reflective surfaces may be attractive but distracting or deceptive. Whether something is broken or intact is also likely to be significant, especially if it is treasured.

LEFT Dreaming of spiral shapes or movement can be an indication of how you feel about your life – is it spiralling out of control, are you on your way up and out, or are you trapped in ever-decreasing circles?

BELOW FAR LEFT Texture can feature in a dream. A feeling of roughness might be threatening but could also be attractive.
BELOW LEFT Curves can suggest freedom and self-expression. If you dream of them perhaps you feel you need less restriction in your life.
BELOW Formal patterns and straight lines might suggest constriction and a lack of imagination, but can bring a feeling of security and comfort if you feel life is too random and out of control.

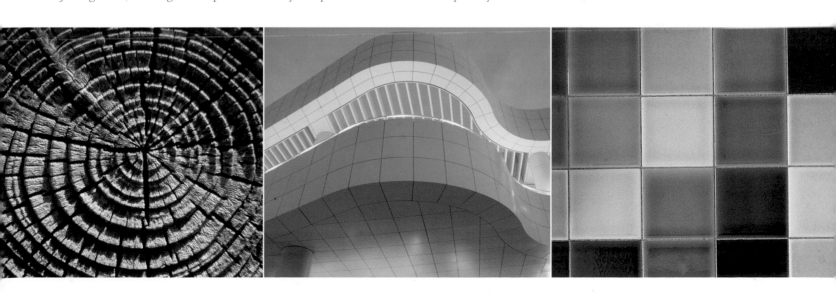

NATURE DREAMS

How we relate to the world around us and how secure we feel about being alive and part of our environment are revealed in dreams of nature. In nature we find the unspoilt, original state of our essential inner being, the truth of who we are as individuals. Landscapes, whether natural or urban, are highly evocative, and set the mood or tone of the dream. Together with the weather, they suggest the atmosphere and underlying impression of your dream, and give clues to your frame of mind, your disposition, your emotional states. The four elements, fire, earth, air and water, work as basic symbols for some key abstract concepts – principally passion, practicality, communication and ideas, and emotions. Animals and plants reveal some of our most primitive, instinctive feelings and fears, which arise from the deepest levels of our unconscious, and from the thoughts and understandings of the world that we formed during the years of our childhood.

DREAM LANDSCAPES

THE LANDSCAPE IS THE BACKDROP FOR THE ACTION OF THE DREAM. IT ANCHORS A DREAM IN TIME AND PLACE AND SETS THE GENERAL THEME AND MOOD, JUST AS SET DESIGN CAN ESTABLISH THE TONE OF A PLAY. CHANGING THE SET OR THE DREAMSCAPE CAN BRING ABOUT A COMPLETELY DIFFERENT EXPERIENCE FOR THE AUDIENCE OR THE DREAMER, EVEN IF THE STORY AND THE CHARACTERS REMAIN THE SAME. AS WELL AS THE PHYSICAL SCENERY ITSELF, THE QUALITY OF THE LANDSCAPE — FAMILIAR OR ALIEN, COMFORTABLE OR DISORIENTATING, OPEN OR RESTRICTED AND CLAUSTROPHOBIC — WILL HAVE EMOTIONAL SIGNIFICANCE AND AFFECT THE GENERAL FEELING OF THE DREAM.

NATURAL LANDSCAPES

Any given landscape can mean different things to different people, and you need to look at both yourself and the context of the dream to understand what it is trying to tell you. Many landscape elements, such as mountains and rivers, have very basic symbolic meanings. For instance, mountains commonly represent obstacles and rivers strong emotional currents. But even if this seems true for you, how you respond to mountains and rivers as well as how you cope with obstacles and emotions will put a personal spin on the dream images. Someone with a fear of heights will see a mountainous landscape quite differently from a mountaineer, and their unconscious will use this image to express quite different things. Even two people who attach the same meaning to mountains may interpret the same dream quite differently if one views obstacles as frightening and daunting and the other as exciting and challenging.

Your position in relation to the landscape is also important – being on top of a mountain and gazing out over a glorious landscape of snow-covered peaks will probably give you an exhilarating sense of achievement, whereas standing at the base and needing to get to the other side may rather bring up feelings associated with challenges as yet unmet. A stream may symbolize something relatively minor that needs to be overcome, and a bridge crossing it could give you a means of getting over that obstacle. Jungles can give rise to a feeling of being lost, alienated, emotional or fearful, but they could create a sense of being at one with the lushness and aliveness of nature in all its abundance. Being in a desert could symbolize barrenness, isolation or disorientation in some aspect of your life, or you may feel relaxed in such a vast open space if you easily feel hemmed in.

Chasms, ravines and abysses in their physical form can be frightening, as one stands on the brink, facing the possibility of falling in or losing things irretrievably over the edge. These

ABOVE What are you doing in your dream? If you are climbing a mountain you might be doing likewise symbolically in your waking life.
RIGHT If you dream of open plains and vast wildernesses then maybe you are feeling lost in your real world.
FAR RIGHT Wide open spaces in your dream could be intimidating, but perhaps means that you feel hemmed in and wish to break free from constriction and restraint.

edges of nature may represent major difficulties you are facing in your everyday waking life, issues that you are afraid to look into a sense of no return.

Beaches provide a transition point between the solidity of terra firma and the vast sea of emotions. They are the threshold of opportunity to enter into deep emotional states, places where you have the freedom to revel in being yourself and recapture the simple joys of childhood.

THE MANUFACTURED LANDSCAPE

Not all landscapes are natural, though. Cities and big towns may symbolize complex problems that have to be negotiated, with straight streets and avenues helping to give you a clear sense of direction. Indeed how roads help or hinder your journey is very telling – if in your dream you find yourself lost in a maze of back streets and alleyways, then perhaps this dream is trying to bring to your attention a sense

of being lost and fearful, while forked paths represent decisions or choices, and twists and turns imply confusion and setbacks. Open roads could leave you feeling exposed and vulnerable on one hand or clear-sighted on the other. Or a road could be hemmed in by walls, fences, high banks or vegetation, giving a feeling of security or claustrophobia. Notice whether you stroll or feel the need to run, and how comfortable you are with the path you are on – it could be symbolizing your path through life.

Walls and fences are also ambiguous symbols. As they can close you in, they may serve as barriers, cutting you off from the rest of the world, or give a sense of security and ownership. Gates also provide openings in otherwise restricted areas, and opportunities to look outward into the unknown from a safe space. Noticing whether you look for a gate or avoid one can give you clues to your emotional state.

LONELINESS DREAM
"In my dream I was walking along a beach. This was no ordinary beach, though – it was located outside of space, a planet floating on its own. I felt unutterably sad there, like I was the last woman left in the universe and there was no one else. It made me realize how lonely I'd been and I resolved to do something about it."

ABOVE Where do you fit into the landscape? Are you part of it or an observer? This is important if you want to know what your dream means. Dreaming of cities and towns may represent complex problems in our life.

FAR LEFT If you dream of a stream try to remember its characteristics, is it bubbling and friendly, does it present an obstacle, is it flowing where you would like to go?
LEFT Are you comfortable in your dream landscape or do you feel alien and out of place; too large or too small?

THE WEATHER

LIKE LANDSCAPES, THE WEATHER COLOURS OUR DREAMS EMOTIONALLY, GIVING BROAD CLUES TO HOW WE FEEL ABOUT OUR
LIVES, AND WHAT SORT OF GENERAL MOOD WE ARE EXPERIENCING IN OUR EVERYDAY WAKING LIVES. WE GENERATE THE
WEATHER IN OUR DREAMS AS A WAY OF EXPRESSING OUR FEELINGS. BECAUSE WHEN WE ARE AWAKE OUR MOODS CAN BE
STRONGLY AFFECTED BY THE WEATHER AND THE SEASON, AND AS THERE ARE MANY WORDS THAT WE USE INTERCHANGEABLY
TO DESCRIBE BOTH THE WEATHER AND OUR MOODS AND FEELINGS (STORMY, GLOOMY, SUNNY, HAZY, TO NAME JUST A FEW),
THESE ARE RELATIVELY EASY SYMBOLS TO START WITH WHEN TRYING TO MAKE SENSE OF OUR DREAMS.

ABOVE Rain may symbolize our problems and worries raining down on us – or it might just be raining in our dream.
ABOVE RIGHT In your dream you may be relaxing, taking time out to enjoy the sunshine. Enjoy this dream holiday.

FAIR OR FOUL?

Moods fluctuate, sometimes unpredictably, in much the same way as the weather. Usually the weather in a dream is congruent with how you are feeling, so calm, sunny weather could indicate a peaceful or happy disposition, while a storm could be expressing anger.

But it is worth taking a closer look at weather that seems to be at odds with your mood. You might be raging in your dream but if the background weather is calm and pleasant you can be fairly certain that your rage will soon pass. On the other hand, if you are being serene and reasonable in your dream but storm clouds are gathering and the temperature dropping, this could be a sign that you need to focus your attention on feelings that are being repressed.

RAIN AND SNOW

As water is widely considered to be a symbol for emotions, rain and tears alike are richly evocative of your emotional state. Grey skies and rain clouds cast a gloomy shadow over your spirit, and could indicate that your unconscious is trying to work with feelings of depression or despondency. You may express your tears as rain – the gentle summer rain that clears the air and feels good, the light drizzle of a spring day, or the deluge of the storm. The rain can be cold and invigorating, or warm and welcoming, and an unexpected shower of rain could mean that you feel your enthusiasm or interest have suddenly been dampened. Any kind of rain can also have a cleansing and rejuvenating effect. Snow can be seen as rain in crystalline form. It

ABOVE Water represents emotions and rain is often linked to tears – if you dream of rain, is there someone you are crying for? If it is a natural expression of grief or tension then you might find a dream of rain is as beneficial as a good cry.

provides another way of expressing emotions, colder and clearer, but also often softer and gentler, and it dramatically changes the appearance of the landscape. It can mean the fun of playtime, but it can also be threatening – blizzards and avalanches show the emotions becoming overwhelming and out of control.

STORMS

In the build-up to a storm, a hush descends on nature along with a feeling of anticipation of the power to be unleashed when the storm breaks. Dark, heavy clouds can be oppressive and threatening, and people who bottle up their emotions will recognize in the calm before the storm the moments before an emotional outburst.

Torrents of rain, dark, heavy clouds, and rumbles or claps of deep thunder all express the charged emotional content of the dream, whether anger or passion or outrage. Because storms can be dramatic, attention-grabbing events, they are likely to be central to the plot of the dream. Having a stormy dream gives you a safe opportunity to play out powerful emotions that may be too difficult or too dangerous to express in real life. Lightning gives dramatic moments of clarity as it illuminates the landscape. The passing of a storm parallels the end of an emotional outburst – you may feel relieved and invigorated by having put out your feelings, or you may be surveying the damage caused.

MIST AND FOG

By contrast, dreaming of mist and fog, drizzle and gloom, all of which obscure the landscape, may suggest that you are unsure of how you feel about something. Pay particular attention to what you do in your dream to clear the air, to see the way forward, as this may give you clues to what you can do in your waking life to resolve a confusing issue. Weather that obscures things can also be hinting that you are in a state of denial about something, and you may need to ask yourself what it is you are not acknowledging.

RIGHT The seasons have their own rhythms which figure largely in our life. Do dark clouds in your dreams presage the coming of winter, or a storm? Does this resonate in your waking life?
MIDDLE RIGHT Nature is a powerful symbol, and a dream of sunshine is likely to hold pleasant connotations. It could also be a nostalgia for a lost golden age.
BOTTOM RIGHT Dreaming of a blanket of snow may symbolize a deadening effect in our waking life – all is cold and forgotten.

THE SEASONS AND THEIR RHYTHMS

The rhythms of nature can be seen in the cycle of the seasons. As the year progresses and the seasons change, the days lengthen and shorten, the weather and the landscape changes, and plants grow, wither and die. These patterns can also have a profound effect on our outlook, behaviour, and lifestyles. The sequence of the seasons can also symbolize the progression from birth to death and the experiences that we have at different times of our lives.

SEASONAL SYMBOLISM
Spring – birth and childhood, a time of innocence, growth, bursting forth, warming and reviving, love and romance.
Summer – youth, vigour, warmth or heat (either giving or sapping energy), abundance, lushness, growth, happiness.
Autumn – maturity, ageing, rich colours and experience, closing in, settling down, preparing for death, reflection.
Winter – old age and death, barrenness, lack of colour, darkness, stillness, isolation, dryness and brittleness, loss.

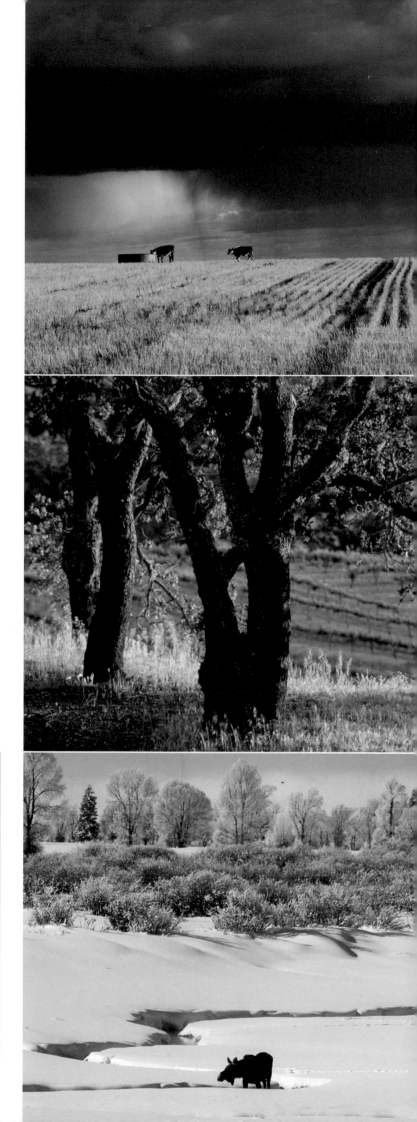

THE ELEMENTS: EARTH

THE ANCIENT GREEK PHILOSOPHERS REGARDED FIRE, EARTH, AIR AND WATER AS PHYSICAL MANIFESTATIONS OF SPIRITUAL ESSENCES. THE PROPERTIES OF THESE FOUR ELEMENTS, AS THEY ARE COLLECTIVELY KNOWN, COULD BE USED TO REPRESENT ABSTRACT CONCEPTS – THE PASSION OF FIRE, THE PRACTICAL AND STABLE NATURE OF EARTH, AIR AS THE MEDIUM FOR THE COMMUNICATION OF IDEAS, AND THE DEEP EMOTIONS OF WATER – AND WERE USED TO UNDERSTAND OUR PHYSICAL AND EMOTIONAL WORLD. THROUGH THE CENTURIES AND IN DIFFERENT CULTURES AROUND THE GLOBE, THESE IDEAS HAVE A MORE OR LESS UNIVERSAL SIGNIFICANCE, AND AS SUCH ARE EXTREMELY IMPORTANT ELEMENTS IN OUR DREAMS.

Earth is where we make our impression: our boot leaves its imprint, and our hands mould and shape it. Earth symbolizes the reality of a situation; it is practical, sensible and stable, and represents conventional, traditional values, long-term goals and ambitions. It is also a powerful symbol for those aspects of our world that are timeless and unchanging. What we make from clay will become mud or dust once again when we have finished with it or discarded it and moved on in our lives. The earth provides the food that sustains us and nurtures us, but is also where we go when we have died, a dark and mysterious place where our physical being gradually disappears.

STABILITY

In our dreams, Earth usually plays a supporting rather than a starring role, and as the only one of the four elements that is solid, it represents stability and passivity. In the form of mud or dry dust, compost, clay or sand, gravel or rocks it can have different qualities; at the grand end of the scale it can even be the whole planet. How it appears as an element in our dream may say a lot about how stable we feel ourselves to be. Fields or meadows, for instance, show that we feel grounded and at peace with ourselves. Conversely, Earth may come to our attention dramatically as an earthquake, a mudslide or quicksand where we can be buried alive. Dreams of eruptions usually mean that our unconscious is troubled – we feel insecure, or fear that we are on the verge of turmoil and upheaval in otherwise stable areas of our lives. Be aware though, that stability taken to an extreme could manifest as rigidity and inflexibility, or as passivity.

MATERIALISM AND THE SENSES

The Earth element is a physical one: it is about holding energy in a material form, about creating, building and augmenting solid things or structures. Because of this, it is also about how we experience those things with our physical bodies – in Jungian terms, it is about sensation. It is likely to feature more in the dreams of people who focus on their body and their physical

LEFT Earth is a very powerful symbol – dust to dust, earth to earth, it's where we feel we come from and where our bodies are returned after our death. How does the earth figure in your own dreams?

ABOVE Flowers and meadows indicate a settled, rooted approach to life.

ABOVE Dreams of fields and farms may also indicate that we feel settled and happy and relaxed enough to enjoy such a dream.

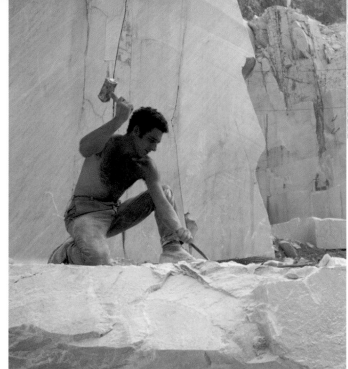

surroundings, or in people who are realistic and pragmatic. We may well ask ourselves if the earth we dream of is being useful; gardening, for instance, shows that we are engaging with it in a practical and creative way, and providing the security of a food supply and a pleasant, nourishing environment.

EARTH AND THE OTHER THREE ELEMENTS

It can be revealing to see how Earth interacts with the other elements in our dreams. The heavy power of physicality found in Earth is the foil to Air's flight of the intellect. Being brought back down to earth means we must engage with reality and practical issues. Air dries out earth, turning wet mud into dust. While passionate fire burns the earth, melting the metals in it, water will turn dust back into mud, enabling seeds to germinate and grow.

By working in harmony with other elements the Earth element is creative in character – it allows the forces of the other elements to work upon it, to alter its dynamics in various ways.

ABOVE Earth is a very creative force but in our dream it may appear as barren or destroyed. We need to look closely at exactly how the Earth element appears.
BELOW Sometimes we need to be earthed, to be grounded, and our dream may be directing us to do this in our waking world.

ABOVE Working the earth in any way may indicate a need to control, to have power over our destiny and fate.
BELOW Do you feel that our planet nurtures us or that you are in control of it? Do you feel it is our mother or our servant?

THE ELEMENTS: FIRE

THE CLASSIC SYMBOL OF PASSION AND VITALITY. FIRE IN A DREAM CAN TAKE MANY FORMS. IT CAN BE THE RAGING BLAZE OF A FOREST FIRE, THE TINY FLAME OF A CANDLE, THE HEAT OF THE MIDDAY SUN IN AFRICA, A ROARING FURNACE OR BONFIRE, AN OPEN LOG FIRE – EVEN A MATCH OR THE GLOWING END OF A LIT CIGARETTE. FIRE IS THE ELEMENT ASSOCIATED WITH OUR NERVOUS SYSTEM AND WITH MOVEMENT. IT IS OUR ENERGY, WHETHER PHYSICAL, EMOTIONAL, CREATIVE OR INTELLECTUAL. WHAT IS BEING BURNT, HOW IT IS BURNING, AND WHETHER IT IS A PRINCIPAL ASPECT OF THE DREAM OR MERELY BACKGROUND ILLUMINATION ALL AFFECT THE MEANING OF THIS SYMBOL.

SHAPES AND FORMS

Many things can produce a flame in our dream. An open log fire may represent romance and intimacy, or it could invoke feelings of comfort, of the warmth and cosiness of long, leisurely winter evenings, a warm haven protected from the cold outdoors. As a symbol of relationships, it can imply the security of a steady, warm love rather than an exciting and unpredictable new passion.

A bonfire, on the other hand, is usually livelier, more convivial and demonstrative. Bonfires are often celebratory events, and mark the purging of dead matter, of the accumulation of clutter in our lives. The ashy remains of an extinguished fire mark the end of a period of energetic activity, or of a passionate relationship.

BELOW Fire is a difficult element – dangerous and unpredictable. How much control we have over it in our dream may indicate how much control we feel we have in life.
BELOW RIGHT Looking at what is burning in our fire dreams may indicate what our fears are in waking life.

CONTROL

Fire is a difficult element, dangerous and unpredictable. How much control you have over the fire may suggest the amount of control you have over a volatile situation or relationship in your waking life. A fire that is out of control may be pointing to a lack of constraint, or to fears about a fraught situation in your life becoming overwhelming or having devastating consequences. Tending a fire may show how we keep control over things, but it could also suggest an urge to interfere with a natural process.

Various agents may have an influence on the meaning of fire. Water quenching the flames or air being blown in to cause an inferno can change how the fire burns and the effects that it has, and so alter its symbolic value.

DESTRUCTION

Fire can often be seen as a destructive and irredeemable force; burning away or acting as a ritualized ending of some aspect or phase of your life. In its positive aspect, it purges, cleanses and purifies.

Whether what is being burned is valued or something you would like to get rid of is central to whether this is a traumatic destruction or one that gives a sense of relief and release. Your response to seeing someone burning books on an open bonfire, for instance, would say a lot about the nature of how you view learning, literature, culture, freedom of speech and so on. Many people prize books, holding them as a valuable source of information, inspiration and entertainment, and would be horrified by such destruction, but a person who cannot read may see this as a liberating dream. The destruction need not be dramatic, though – even blowing out a candle can symbolize the extinguishing of something.

ILLUMINATION

Fire also brings light and hope, dispelling darkness and revealing aspects of your life that need uncovering, bringing them to light. The steady flame of the candle gives constant illumination but little warmth, while a bonfire flares up and burns fiercely, casting great dancing shadows, then dies down again when its flames are spent. How it burns and how much attention you give it can tell you about areas of your relationships that you may need to work on.

CREATIVITY

The fire in a kiln or furnace or forge is immensely hot, and yet it is contained and controlled, and we put it to use to create things, both functional and aesthetic, that enhance our lives. We also use fire to prepare food. In these senses we can understand it as an expression of our creativity and productivity. By adding fuel to a fire we are giving our creativity greater expression.

SMOKE

A by-product of fire, smoke can be toxic or suffocating, making you ill or unable to breathe, and polluting the environment. As such it could be trying to bring to your attention the need to escape from a suffocating or unhealthy relationship before it destroys you. If there is a lot of smoke you may have difficulty seeing your way forward.

In a positive sense though, smoke signals could be giving you a message, showing you where the fire can be found or warning you away from it, and the smell of a fire or incense can bring good associations or be used deliberately to enhance your mood and bring about a feeling of stillness.

LEFT Fire can be warm and comforting as well as dangerous and unpredictable, a cosy fireside scene in your dream can be a totally unthreatening image. **MIDDLE LEFT** Fire can be controlled and is also vital as a tool for our wellbeing and comfort. Dreaming of fire that is under your power and is being used in some way can indicate a level of empowerment in life. **BOTTOM LEFT** Fire in the form of the small quiet fire of the candle can symbolize the tiny flame of spiritual progress.

THE ELEMENTS: AIR

AIR IS THE VERY BREATH OF LIFE: WITHOUT IT WE SUFFOCATE AND DIE. IT HAS NO FORM, SUBSTANCE, SHAPE OR TEXTURE AND YET IT SURROUNDS US, REPRESENTING FREEDOM AND SPACE AND OPENNESS, BOTH IN A LITERAL WAY AND IN THE SENSE OF FREE AND OPEN COMMUNICATION. IT FILLS OUR LUNGS, GIVING US THE CAPACITY TO BREATHE, SPEAK, SING AND SHOUT – TO EXPRESS OUR EMOTIONS. AS ONE OF THE FOUR ELEMENTS, IT RELATES TO THE MIND AND THE INTELLECT, THE GENERATION AND COMMUNICATION OF IDEAS. WE CAN'T SEE AIR OR WIND, BUT WE CAN FEEL AND SEE ITS EFFECTS – DRIFTS OF SMOKE, LEAVES STIRRING, TREES BENT IN A GALE, CLOUDS SCUDDING BY OVERHEAD, BUBBLES IN WATER.

ABOVE We might not be able to see the air but we can see the creatures that use it and fly in it. If we dream of them, perhaps we are envying their soaring energy and freedom.

The current of air, whether it is a breeze or hurricane, is a vehicle for self-expression – like the air, our thoughts and emotions too are invisible but their effect is all too apparent at times. Smells are carried on the air, providing information about our environment and often generating an instant emotional response in us.

We should also look at how Air works in conjunction with the other three elements. Without air the fire cannot burn. Earth, water and air, together with the sun's

warmth and light, bring forth plants that sustain all living creatures on our planet.

THE INTELLECT
Traditionally, the element of Air symbolizes the intellect and our powers of communication. How clear the air is in our dream may show how clearly we are giving and receiving visual information and sounds. "Hot air" is a term meaning excessive verbiage, and we could see this as intellectual clutter. The mind does pick up puns, so dreams of hot air

ABOVE We can now use the air for recreational sports and doing so in our dreams could make us feel liberated and free. A dream of flying might mean we yearn for space and freedom.

ballooning, for instance, or jets of hot air, could well suggest communication overload to you – not surprising in this information age.

WIND
Air is often manifest as wind, and in our dream we should look at what effect it is having, what role

it is playing. Is it sustaining and helping us, like a cool breeze on a hot day? Do we work with it – flying, soaring or being borne aloft by it – or is it a powerful and harmful force, like the strong winds of a storm that blow us flat and bring destruction in their wake? As a symbol of intellectual and emotional direction and force, the wind in your dream is an outward manifestation of your internal life.

SUFFOCATION

The lack of air is usually more noticeable than its presence, and suffocation is an important dream theme. Suffocating, feeling short of breath, or even being in a stuffy room may show that our emotional and spiritual expression is being stifled, or that our intellect is not being

exercised sufficiently. Likewise, if we are ourselves choking someone or something, this may be pointing to unconscious guilt at choking the life out of a relationship, not allowing another person enough space and freedom, not saying what we want to say or not giving the other an opportunity to speak and be heard.

OBSCURITY

Smoke, haze or mist all obscure the view, suggesting a lack of clarity in your thinking, or being unable to see your way forward. Equally, debris flying through the air could indicate distractions, a whirl of ideas, or being caught up with other people's ideas.

HOLY BREATH

As we breathe we feel the air entering and leaving our body. The Hindus talk of *prana* – holy breath, cosmic spirit. The same is true of the Taoists of China who speak of *ch'i* – again a cosmic spirit or energy that flows like air

– and feng shui – literally "wind and water", the two cosmic forces that shape the landscape in which we live and bring us health and life. In the Bible, the Holy Spirit is said to manifest in several forms, including as a wind and a flame.

AN AIR DREAM

"I was standing on a high hill with the wind blowing all around me. Then suddenly I was being shot upwards at tremendous speed through a plastic tube on a column of air. In a flash the hill was far below me, getting smaller and smaller, more and more distant. I was aware of how important the air was. It was holding me, shooting me upwards. Without it I would fall back to the earth again and be killed.

As I realized I was reaching the top of the column I woke up and remember feeling incredibly grateful for the dream, and that I had to learn to breathe more deeply, to feel more alive."

BELOW Wind can be frightening and destructive as well as dangerous, and our dreams can reflect our fears of the untameable, wild and erratic manifestation of air.

BELOW LEFT The wind blowing through grasses is an evocative image. Are you dreaming of bending to forces that you find irresistible?
BELOW Smoke rising in misty swirls can be linked with holy breath, our spirit selves.

THE ELEMENTS: WATER

WATER HAS LONG BEEN THOUGHT OF AS THE SYMBOLIC VEHICLE OF EXPRESSION FOR OUR EMOTIONS, FEELINGS AND SENSITIVITY. IT IS, IN FACT, A PERFECT SYMBOL FOR THESE AS THE FORMS IT TAKES ARE SO VARIED. WATER IS THE SAME SUBSTANCE WHETHER IT IS A STILL POOL, A RAGING TORRENT, TOWERING WAVES ON THE BEACH, OR A DRIPPING TAP AT HOME. WITH THE SAME WIDE SPECTRUM, EMOTIONS CAN RANGE FROM SORROW, ANGER, JEALOUSY AND BEREAVEMENT, TO JOY, EXCITEMENT AND LOVE. ANY KIND OF WATER IMAGE IN A DREAM HOLDS THE POTENTIAL TO SYMBOLIZE OUR EMOTIONS AND OUR EMOTIONAL NEEDS, DESIRES AND CAPABILITIES.

BELOW Water is very evocative. It has a great power to move us, causes us to dream, and makes us reflective and contemplative. Eddying brooks and small streams are soothing, and to dream of any of these is a sign that we are relaxed and comfortable.
BELOW RIGHT The more we try to hold on to water – to our emotions and tears – the more it escapes from us; it is elusive and fluid.

Water represents the full range of different emotions, and it is immensely difficult to generalize when analysing the symbolism of water images. A scene that for some may be scary – say, a raging sea on a stormy night – might for someone else be exciting and exhilarating. Similarly, while for some people it is enough to feel emotionally comfortable and stable, others seek passion and new challenges.

BODIES OF WATER

Vast and deep, the sea is a particularly useful symbol for the enormity of our unplumbed, unconscious emotional depths. In some respects it is always changing, with the weather and with the ebb and flow of the tides and the constant movement of the great ocean currents – and yet it has its own rhythm and predictable aspects.

Rivers represent our emotional journey and can show us whether we let our emotions flow easily. Whether the river in your dream is strong and fast-flowing, a babbling brook or a brackish backwater could well be saying something about the strength of your emotions, and whether you are allowing them to be expressed fully and in a healthy way. Do you go with the flow, or swim against the current? Crossing a river may indicate that your emotions present some kind of obstacle, so having a means of doing so – a bridge, a raft, a ford – could be showing that there is a way forward. The stillness of a pool or pond can show the peace and tranquillity of a steady, reflective nature. A lagoon may provide a haven of stillness from the open sea without breaking contact with your emotional nature, and the protective, enclosing nature of the lagoon suggests a feminine aspect.

QUALITY AND QUANTITY

Our lives depend on water, but it must be pure to sustain and clean us. Dreaming of muddied, stagnant or polluted water may indicate that our emotions are confused or unhealthy, even harmful, and we may need to pay special attention to looking after ourselves, giving ourselves enough space to know what we are really feeling, and not engage in self-negativity.

A deluge may be completely overwhelming, and can wipe out everything in its path, but water also evaporates, and the lack of it can equally be traumatic. Being profoundly thirsty or in a dry, barren place can indicate that our emotional side is neglected and is in need of reviving.

RELATIONSHIP TO WATER

Where are you in relation to the water in your dream, and how do you respond to it? You may be beside a body of water trying to skirt it, crossing it in a boat, or dithering about whether to get in, or perhaps you can't wait to take a running dive and feel the rush of bubbles past your skin. If you find yourself already in the water, are you floating, sinking or swimming? You may see water as a place to have fun, a place where you can be mesmerized by the easy, rhythmical movement of your body, or a terrifying place where you feel out of your depth or fear you will drown or be eaten alive.

BELOW Water can be exhilarating; if you dream of pounding waves, perhaps you are wishing for more excitement in your life?

A WATER DREAM

"I was trying desperately to turn off a tap but the water just kept gushing out. I put my hands over the tap but the water seeped out between my fingers. I woke up crying because I recently got divorced and I miss my husband so much. The water in my dreams represented my unstoppable tears."

We use water in a very practical way. Drinking it and cooking with it are positive, embracing tasks that nourish us, while washing ourselves and our possessions in it may indicate a need to rid ourselves of negativity and emotional debris. Dissolving things in water brings about complete transformation.

BIRTH, SEX AND LOVE

We are essentially made of water, and for the first nine months of our existence, the most sheltered, protected time of our lives, we live in fluid. We may be remembering or making sense of this experience when we dream of enclosed water or of being submerged. We talk of the waters breaking just before birth, when we are ready to make our traumatic journey into the world. Fountains, hosepipes, geysers and so on can act as symbols of sexuality – in an obvious way they represent ejaculation, but in a more general sense they can be seen as metaphors for sexual energy and release. A dream of swimming with a lover, for example, may be sensuous in a more tranquil way, and speak of

the harmony of love as you move together in a slow, easy rhythm, at one in a buoyant medium.

TEARS

Dissolving in tears as salty as the sea, we express our sadness, grief, anger, tiredness, fear and insecurity, and in so doing, find emotional release. Many people have taught themselves not to cry, so dreaming of doing so may be particularly powerful if it breaks a personal taboo. If someone else is crying in your dreams, consider whether this is an aspect of yourself that is trying to be expressed.

ABOVE Water dreams might contain water that has been harnessed as a resource, in the form of running taps or over-flowing bathtubs – or perhaps a lack of water, as in dry wells. All could have links with your waking life.

THE PLANT KINGDOM

ABOVE Trees have always had the power to move us, fill us with wonder and awe.
ABOVE RIGHT Trees symbolize the power of nature and growth.

WITH ROOTS THAT SPREAD THROUGH THE DARK, FERTILE EARTH, AND LEAVES AND BRANCHES REACHING TO THE SKY FOR LIGHT AND WARMTH, PLANTS ARE PERFECT SYMBOLS OF THE RICH WORKINGS OF THE HUMAN MIND. LIKE THE UNCONSCIOUS, A PLANT'S ROOTS ARE DARK AND HIDDEN FROM VIEW, YET CAN STILL BE NURTURED WITH WATER AND FOOD, AND CAN PRODUCE A HEALTHY PLANT ABOVE GROUND. BRANCHES, LEAVES AND FLOWERS ARE THE VISIBLE MANIFESTATIONS OF OUR MINDS, AND TELL US ABOUT OUR MENTAL AND EMOTIONAL HEALTH.

LEFT The tree as a symbol of life, with its head in the sky and its roots buried in the earth, is deeply buried in our consciousness and permeates most cultures on earth with its resonance.

TREES

Rooted deep in our unconscious and in the emotional landscape of our dreams, trees are often regarded as symbols of the past – of steady growth, age, experience, time and continuity.

Using this concept, we can see a wood as our family history and forests as the history of our society, culture, or ethnic group. Roots provide wisdom from the collective experience, and how you view trees may indicate how you feel about your own "roots".

Some tree species hold particular symbolic value, and around the world have long been valued as sacred or politically powerful icons. The oak, for instance, is seen as a symbol of longevity, strength, reliability and resilience. Down the ages the willow has had connotations of death or enchantment, and the evergreen holly with its scarlet berries has brought hope and cheer in the dark of winter. In ancient Britain certain trees were chosen as totems or symbols of tribal power – if one tribe ousted another, they uprooted a tree of the vanquished tribe and thrust it upside-down into the ground as a show of dominance. Such symbols may have lost relevance, but they are still embedded in our cultural consciousness and reappear in our dreams.

One of the key visual and conceptual symbols of the Jewish Kabbalah, used to investigate the mysteries of our spiritual life and

ABOVE Harvested food has many symbolic meanings. A cornucopia of produce can mean growth, plenty, vitality and sufficiency.

our relationship with God, is the complex diagram of the Tree of Life. A similar idea is used in the mythology of Native American Indian people, where the tree of life is what links heaven to earth. Shamans use this imagery in their journeys between worlds, and in their interpretation of dreams.

FLOWERS AND VINES

Associated with pleasure, beauty and relaxation, flowers also denote giving and receiving. Cultivated garden flowers imply order and the application of discipline over creativity, while wild flowers are much more intuitive and express our artistic leanings. Dead flowers may indicate a need to look at underlying unhappiness. Climbing plants may show a need to escape from a situation, or a feeling of entanglement. Some, such as honeysuckle, clematis and vines, are said to represent our ambitions.

FRUIT AND VEGETABLES

Ripe, juicy, seed-laden fruit is associated with fertility and readiness. Apples have associations of seductiveness because of the biblical temptation in the Garden of Eden, but equally they may symbolize the autumn, or the fruitfulness of our maturing unconscious. Over-ripe fruit may signify a loss of fertility, or a wasted opportunity.

Dreaming of vegetables shows a concern with nourishment, fullness and abundance – or the lack of those qualities if they are dried out or of poor quality. The shape of some vegetables may suggest sexuality, although the context of your dream will tell you whether this is true for you.

GARDENING

Dreams about gardening may show you how you feel about work and career issues. Work and gardening alike may seem fulfilling or drudgery. We respond to gardens emotionally and the colour they bring into our lives, but weeds can choke out and destroy the life of our garden and distract us from its beauty. They may show that there are problems in our working life that need to be eliminated.

ABOVE If you dream of flowers you should try to remember their setting – are they contained within a controlled garden, or are they growing wild?
ABOVE LEFT What does a garden rose mean to you, natural beauty or excessive cultivation?

GARDEN DREAMS

If you have a gardening dream it is worth looking at what you are doing and how you are doing it, to give you clues to how you approach the practical aspects of your life.

Digging Preparing the groundwork

Weeding and pest control Removing elements, allowing desirable elements to grow unhindered

Planting Nurturing, creating opportunities

Harvesting Reaping the benefits

Grass cutting Vital maintainance work

CREATURES OF THE LAND

ANIMALS SHOW US OUR MORE INNOCENT, INSTINCTIVE AND INTUITIVE SELVES. THEY SHOW US HOW WE MIGHT BE IF THE RESTRAINTS AND TABOOS WE LEARN THROUGHOUT OUR LIVES WERE REMOVED, AND THE VENEER OF CIVILIZATION, MATURITY AND SOPHISTICATION STRIPPED AWAY. OUR PLAYFULNESS AND CURIOSITY, AGGRESSION AND SEXUALITY MAY ALL BE EXPRESSED IN OUR DREAMS THROUGH IMAGES OF ANIMALS. OF COURSE WHAT EACH ANIMAL SYMBOLIZES WILL VARY FROM CULTURE TO CULTURE. IT IS EASY FOR URBAN WESTERNERS TO SAY A LION REPRESENTS STRENGTH, WHEN TO AN AFRICAN LIVING IN THE BUSH IT MIGHT JUST SYMBOLIZE DANGER AND FEAR.

CHARACTERISTICS

If there are strong cultural associations or stereotypes around an animal's character, such as the stealth of a tiger or the cunning of the fox, you may bring the animal into your dream to stand in for such meanings, but if it is a less distinguished creature or one you don't recognize, it could be its wildness, or some characteristic or behaviour it is exhibiting in your dream, that is important. Such characteristics show you something about yourself, characteristics that you should aspire to, or avoid, or eliminate. Whether the animal is behaving normally or doing something odd

or bizarre, may say how comfortable you are with what the animal represents, or that its natural qualities are present but are being subverted.

ASSOCIATIONS

When you dream of an animal, see what associations it has for you, as well as if there are any stereotypes around that animal. Baby animals often have different associations from those of the adult, but also bear the characteristics of the adult. Use the list provided to spark off your own ideas.

WILD ANIMALS

Freud held that dreams of wild animals represent our unbridled passions – lust, greed, jealousy and the like. It is possible that the animal in your dream represents your sexual fears (a bull or a stallion the loss of prowess, a crow unfaithfulness) but such a prescriptive interpretation fails to take into account either the characteristics of the animal or the personal response you have to it. It may make more sense to extend Freud's interpretation of wild animals to mean our unbridled nature – wild animals in their natural habitat are unconstrained, so like other elements of nature, they show us some aspect of our

true selves. In a zoo or cage, farm or game reserve, the animal is to a greater or lesser extent enclosed – for display, consumption or its own protection – and its natural impulses may be curbed. If the animal in your dream has been contained like this, see whether it is content or fretting, aggressive or apathetic, to understand your own relationship with being constrained. A wild animal being hunted may suggest a threat to your natural self, while an animal stalking or hunting may have connotations of strategy, self-sufficiency or single-mindedness.

PETS

The animals in our dreams are often domestic rather than wild animals, and our familiarity with our pets is likely to give us a greater feel for their range of characteristics. If the animal is our own pet, we may relate to it more like a family member than an animal, as we know its behaviours and moods intimately and have a strong emotional bond. Your pet's playful, devoted, aloof or mysterious nature may be what you are trying to work with in your dream.

FARMING

Farm animals have qualities of both wildness and domesticity, but the relevant characteristics of

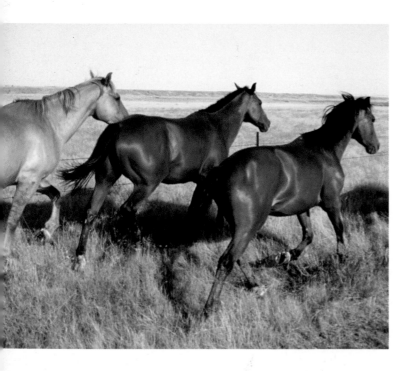

BELOW What are the animals in your dream doing? Their behaviour is as important as what kind of beast they are.

these creatures may be that they are bred and reared for slaughter; they live in vast herds or flocks or stacked up in sheds, and they are contained in a limited and sometimes very unnatural environment. This processing of animals may seem acceptable to you, or you may regard it with ambivalence or abhorrence; your attitude will influence the meaning of the dream.

RIGHT Most animal symbolism is fairly easy to interpret – sweet cuddly lambs are exactly that.
MIDDLE RIGHT Some animal symbolism is more complex, and carries cultural resonances – is this lion a symbol of power? Strength? Danger? Does it attract or repel you?
BOTTOM RIGHT To someone who lives where deer roam free, a dream of stags locking their antlers may denote passion and fertility, whereas to people who are divorced from the reality it might symbolize aggression and violence.

SPIDERS AND INSECTS

Tiny and alien in appearance, spiders and insects have quite a different set of meanings which often have little to do with their ability to harm us by stinging or biting us or spreading disease. Many people fear or dislike them at the best of times, often apparently irrationally, and in our dreams they can be monstrous and terrifying.

Spiders weave invisible webs to entrap their unsuspecting prey, so we may use both the spider or the web in our dreams to symbolize being trapped or betrayed in some way. Insects such as bees and ants live in colonies, and so teamwork is vital to their very survival. On its own a tiny insect may seem like nothing much, but collectively they can move large objects, build complex structures and strip a forest bare, providing powerful images for the value of co-operation and the lack of individuation. Insects also seem constantly active, so your dream may suggest a need to slow down, or to be more efficient.

ANIMALS AS FAMILIARS OR MESSENGERS

In some cultures animals are believed to come to people in their dreams as spirit messengers, and the shaman will identify a person's "familiar" – the animal most likely to communicate with them. It could be interesting to see if there is one particular animal that keeps cropping up in your dreams, and whether it communicates any message.

ANIMAL MEANINGS

Lion Raw strength, power, danger, pride, kingship

Dog Devotion, faithfulness

Cat Independence, mystery, love of comfort, hunting

Horse Intelligence, athleticism, strength, nobility

Butterfly Beauty, capriciousness, transformation

Cow Calm, slowness, maternity

Monkey Playfulness, mischief

Mule Stubbornness, bearing of loads

Rabbit Prolific breeding

Snake Deceitfulness, venomousness

Pig Greed, dirtiness

CREATURES OF SKY AND OCEAN

ABOVE Brightly coloured birds are used in our dreams to represent pride and conceit, power and strength.
ABOVE RIGHT The eagle is king of the birds and can therefore represent military might.
ABOVE FAR RIGHT Flocks of birds may represent how we see our own individuality – lost in such vast numbers and part of a crowd, or intact no matter what?

FLYING HIGH IN THE SKY OR SWIMMING DEEP IN THE VAST, COLD WATERS OF THE OCEAN, BIRDS AND FISH ARE CREATURES THAT ARE IN THEIR ELEMENT IN PLACES WE CANNOT EASILY GO. THEIR PHYSICAL CHARACTERISTICS — WINGS AND FINS, FEATHERS AND SCALES, BEAKS AND GILLS — TOGETHER WITH THE LAYING OF EGGS AND THE ABILITY OF BOTH BIRDS AND FISH TO MOVE APPARENTLY EFFORTLESSLY, MAY ALSO HOLD THE KEY TO THEIR APPEARANCE IN OUR DREAMS.

BIRD BEHAVIOURS
The most obvious aspect of bird behaviour, and the one that may most frequently find its way into our dreams, is flight. For us earthbound humans, the ability to fly without the assistance of any craft is as appealing as it is impossible. It represents freedom and hope – the ability to flex our muscles and feel the rush of air as we soar to great heights or cover vast distances on the wing. A "flight of ideas" alludes to a rush of intellectual creativity; on the other hand we speak of "flapping" to mean being in a panic, a feeling of loss of control. Either way, the "birds' eye view" gives us a perspective not normally available to us in which we can see the whole picture.

Back on the ground, birds are perhaps less idealized creatures – their constant pecking and scratching around in the dirt suggest fussing with details, or looking for small rewards, while a "henpecked" husband suffers the constant verbal irritation and bullying of his partner.

The fact that many phrases pertaining to birds and their behaviours have found their way into our language shows how strongly we feel about them, and means that we may incorporate them into our dreams as metaphors for our thoughts, ideas, feelings and behaviour.

NESTS AND EGGS
Birds' nests are often used to symbolize the cosiness and security of a home, and in the phrase "the nesting instinct" we suggest both the idea of settling down and preparing for a family. Nests represent a nurturing environment where the young can be kept safe until maturity, and fend for themselves. A nest may also have the less alluring meaning of a small, messy space. Birds' eggs hint at creation and conception, or more figuratively, the germ of an idea.

BIRDS OF A FEATHER
Particular species of bird have come to have specific meanings, usually by virtue of their character or appearance, or in a few cases because they have found their way into our cultural vocabulary.

Dove Peace, the Holy Spirit

Crow Death

Ostrich Being in denial, "burying your head in the sand" so as not to see important truths

Eagle King of the birds, military victory; symbol of American nationhood

Dodo Extinction

Robin Christmas

Blackbird and nightingale Joyful song

Parrot Speech, imitation

Owl Wisdom

Peacock Brilliance, pride, showing off

All birds of prey Ruthlessness, clearsightedness

FISH

Cold and sleek and silent, fish are creatures of the water and hence are likely to be connected to our emotional states. In their silent world they have an air of mystery about them, and the deeper they reside in the sea, the more frightening and unknowable they often seem. In the murky depths we cannot see far, and we may fear the unknown monsters there as we sometimes fear the most deeply buried parts of our unconscious.

In a fish bowl, however, fish may take on a whole new meaning. Here they are on display; they have nowhere to go and nowhere to hide, and their natural characteristics are changed. In a bowl or aquarium, a fish may signify a feeling of being exposed, and possibly the boredom of a limited and monotonous environment.

The fish is a motif that appears frequently in the Christian tradition, and was used as a secret symbol of association by the early Christians; to this day it may be a sign of faith for some.

CAPTIVITY

Birds in cages and fish in aquariums or bowls are possessed, displayed, and their freedom and natural expression curtailed. Their company is decided by the person who keeps them, and they may be unable to mate. Birds may have their wings clipped, and this too is a sign of restriction and immobility.

Killing a bird may indicate that some lofty ideal is being shot down, or a freedom lost, while hooking a fish could be a sign that some deep-seated emotion has been drawn to the surface.

GROUPS AND NUMBERS

Encountering birds or fish on their own in a dream may suggest the aspirations of the individual, but often we will find birds in flocks and fish in teeming schools, where all sense of individuality is erased in favour of safety and sociability. Issues of co-operation may predominate.

A farm scene may allow for more individuality, but the existence of a pecking order may be marked. Dreaming of pairs of birds could allude to finding a mate and settling down.

ABOVE Dolphins have an extra level of meaning for many cultures. Their high intelligence and charm makes us feel they have an affinity with humans.
ABOVE LEFT What sort of fish appear in our dreams may represent how we feel emotionally about our deepest spiritual life.

BELOW Fish are creatures of the deep, the hidden and the secret, so their symbolism can be quite easy to read. A shoal of fish might indicate how you feel about your position in a social group.

THE CYCLE OF LIFE

No matter who or what we are, we all go through the same cycle of life, from birth through childhood, youth, maturity and old age to death. And no matter how we approach these different stages – whether we enjoy and welcome them or resent and try to avoid them – they are all inevitable, unless we die prematurely. How they appear in our dreams will reflect how enjoyable or difficult we find the whole experience, and dreams about the rites of passage associated with the different stages in the life cycle – about puberty, leaving home, getting married, having children, or retirement, for instance – affect all of us and show how we are in ourselves, whether we feel secure and at ease with where we are in life, or resentful and in denial. Indeed, these dreams are often the way we prepare mentally and emotionally for approaching rites of passage. They may prompt us to ask some of the serious questions about our existence that we may otherwise avoid – about those stages we have yet to go through, and especially about what happens to us when we die.

BIRTH DREAMS

BIRTH IS A HIGHLY SYMBOLIC THEME WHEN IT OCCURS IN OUR DREAMS, AND IT IS ONE WHOSE MEANING IS USUALLY QUITE EASILY INTERPRETED – IT IS ABOUT ORIGINS, NEW BEGINNINGS, LABOURING, THE STRUGGLE FOR INDIVIDUATION AND DEVELOPMENT. OUR OWN BIRTH IS PROBABLY THE MOST MOMENTOUS EVENT OF OUR LIVES, YET VIRTUALLY NO-ONE IS ABLE TO REMEMBER ANYTHING OF IT. IT IS POSSIBLE THOUGH, THAT WE DO RETAIN SOME OF THE SENSE OF IT, THAT THE EXPERIENCE OF IT STAYS WITH US SUBCONSCIOUSLY OUR WHOLE LIFE. WHAT WE ARE TOLD ABOUT IT BY OUR PARENTS OR BY OTHERS WHO WERE PRESENT MAY ALSO AFFECT US DEEPLY.

BEING BORN

In dreams of your own birth it may be that your unconscious is trying to draw your attention to some momentous event that it feels is in some way as traumatic as your birth. Often the dream will give you the clues you need to decipher what this event is – if it is not already immediately obvious. The context of the birth in your dream, together with the feelings you experience around it, will probably reflect how your unconscious feels about the event in your life – apprehensive, excited, hesitant, or reluctant, perhaps – and your unconscious is trying to encourage you to look at why these feelings are

coming up. Birth involves a momentous transition, and we may use it in our dreams to represent the shock of the new, the move into an uncertain and unsafe new world, but one that is full of potential.

As well as giving us the wherewithal to look at important events in the present, dreams about our own birth may also point to feelings or problems buried deep in our psyche. If we were abandoned at birth, or if for some reason we believe that our birth was a disappointment to our parents, we may carry this sense of being abandoned or of not being good enough with us all our lives.

OUR CHILDREN'S BIRTH

Men and women alike may feel apprehensive about their own child being born; this is a major event that brings immense change and responsibility to a person's life, and to dream of it is natural. But women in particular are visited by dreams of birth when they are expecting a child. Such dreams are a way of coming to terms with the new being that is developing inside a woman's own body, and preparing for the birth, as well as for the huge lifestyle changes that happen after the baby arrives. Fears that the unborn child will be somehow less than perfect are quite common, and this fear

BIRTH DREAM

"When I was about six months pregnant I dreamed of a space ship, all silver and spinning, with lots of portholes. It didn't land, but a ladder was lowered and a creature appeared, with spindly arms and legs and big eyes, a bit like the alien at the end of the film 'Close Encounters of the Third Kind'. The alien spoke to me and then somehow entered my belly. I think this dream was my way of accepting that something unknown was growing inside of me, and that I was approaching a new situation I had never been faced with before."

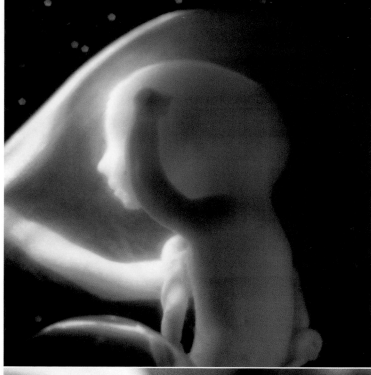

often manifests in dreams about giving birth to a monster or a changeling. Dreams of giving birth may also simply be a wish fulfilment if you want a child.

To dream of our child's birth long after the event may show we are worrying about them for some reason – perhaps they are going through transition, or we are worried about their progress.

BIRTH SYMBOLISM

Dreaming of birth or babies may have nothing to do with real life pregnancy or having babies, but can symbolize a variety of things, such as ideas, projects and plans for the future. A normal birth in a dream may symbolize new beginnings. But if the birth is premature or unnatural we should look at why events are not unfolding in the natural way. Perhaps there is some obstruction and we are too impatient for nature to take its course, forcing it to make its journey into the world prematurely. If this is the case, perhaps you are making something happen without adequate preparation, or putting pressure on someone to start something they are not ready for.

If the creature that is born is unnatural or deformed, this may well be related to stumbling blocks or problems in plans you have made; the nature of its deformity or the qualities that make it unusual are probably significant, so remember as much detail as you can. If you dream of a stillbirth you might be thinking about a project that won't come to fruition, while an abortion may be the plan's termination.

LEFT Dreaming of a baby in the womb could be reflecting your present circumstances, but might have nothing to do with babies at all. Perhaps it reflects ambitious plans and projects in your waking life that you feel need nurturing and bringing to life.
MIDDLE LEFT It is only natural to have lots of birthing drams while pregnant – we all worry about a successful and happy delivery.
BOTTOM LEFT Dreaming of babies can mean that you are dreaming of the growth and maturing of something that is dear to your heart.

CHILDHOOD DREAMS

AS WE GROW UP WE ARE INFLUENCED BY MANY THINGS. THE PEOPLE IN OUR LIVES – ESPECIALLY OUR PARENTS AND SIBLINGS – AS WELL AS THE ENVIRONMENT WE GROW UP IN AND THE COUNTLESS EXPERIENCES WE HAVE DURING OUR CHILDHOOD YEARS, ARE ALL FORMATIVE INFLUENCES, GIVING SHAPE TO OUR PERSONALITY AND THE WAY WE APPROACH THE WORLD. HOW WE REMEMBER OUR CHILDHOOD WILL INFLUENCE HOW WE SEE THIS STAGE OF LIFE IN OUR DREAMS. WHEN WE DREAM OF CHILDREN WE MIGHT BE DREAMING OF OUR OWN CHILDHOOD, BUT WE MIGHT ALSO BE DREAMING OF THE CHILD WE STILL ARE. DREAMS OF CHILDREN MIGHT ALSO SYMBOLIZE IDEAS AND PLANS WE HAVE THAT HAVE YET TO MATURE.

BELOW Dreaming that we are a child again may tell us a lot about how we feel about being grown ups,. Even if the dream is playful it may suggest feelings of unease or feeling ill equipped.

The terrifying moments of our childhood, the pain and trauma that we experience as we grow up get imprinted on our psyche and can scar us for the rest of our lives, surfacing in our dreams even when we are adults, and have "forgotten" the events. Alternatively it could be the freedom of childhood that we are yearning for in our dreams, a time when we could play to our heart's content, a time without the responsibilities and problems we face as adults. Childishness – silly, petty behaviour – may also be expressed in our dreams.

TOYS AND GAMES
Voices from our early years, familiar old toys and memories of games we used to play may all figure in our dreams as symbols of our childhood. This is a time to discover, and much of our learning is done through play, not only with toys and games but also by entering the world of make-believe through dressing-up and role play. These objects and activities are powerfully symbolic and thus easy for your unconscious to choose as representations of childhood – of fun and naivety, of curiosity, growth and development.

Particular toys or scenes may have a special meaning for you, for instance if you dream that your favourite toy, from which you were inseparable as a child, is lost or taken away from you, it could be that your unconscious is using this as an analogy for possession or attachment, separation or grieving, or for a loss of security.

Games involving fantasy and role play could be a hint that we need to be more creative, see life from a different perspective, or try to change how we handle problems. Many children's games rely heavily on rules, and how the game is played can be as important as what is being played – making or breaking the rules, changing them as you go along, cheating or following them rigidly may say something about your relationship to laws and social expectations.

DREAMING OF CHILDREN

When we dream of a child or childishness we might be dreaming of the emotions we link to childhood. Young children are often more expressive than adults, and feel less constrained by what others think when they want to cry or laugh or scream. They have the time and the freedom to play actively and to explore the things they enjoy or find interesting, and may also become completely immersed in the worlds they read about. On the other hand, children may be ignored when they speak, or punished for being noisy or angry, for making a mess or not sitting still.

When we dream of children we might be recalling something in our waking life that makes us feel in a way that we associate with the state of childhood, or we may be echoing something in our everyday life that has given us the status of a child in some way.

ADULTS AS CHILDREN

If we dream about someone else as a child we might be trying to find out what makes them tick, or perhaps to get to the root of why they are the way they are. Suppose you dream of your boss as a child. You may be trying to understand what motivates them, or be attempting to reduce them to someone smaller and less powerful in order to make them less intimidating. You may equally turn an adult into a child in your dream because you want to attempt to exert some kind of control over them, or perhaps because you want to relate to them in a more direct and childlike way.

ABOVE If you dream of a teddy bear does it make you feel nostalgic for your lost childhood?

ABOVE LEFT Children are precious and usually very endearing and it is only natural to dream of such a wonderful gift.

ABOVE FAR LEFT To dream of toys can mean many things and you need to think carefully about the details of your dream, did the toy belong to you? was it broken, desirable, boring, symbolic?

A CHILDHOOD DREAM

"I was upstairs in a small room filled with sunlight, which streamed in through an open window. It was late afternoon towards the end of summer, and I was sitting on the floor, very still, very quiet. I'd been told that I had to stay here, and I had the feeling that something terrible would happen if I didn't.

I didn't understand the dream until I mentioned it to my sister. She told me that our mother would send me to my room when her parents came to visit, as they didn't know she had an illegitimate child and she was afraid they would disinherit her if they found out. She would tell me to go upstairs and stay there, and pretend that I didn't exist. When I heard this I cried and cried. Even though I hadn't remembered my mother doing this it must have made a huge impression on me, as all my life I've felt like I had to be bigger and better than anyone else – and make sure everyone knows I'm there! I like to think that the sunshine and the open window show my unstoppable outgoing nature, which existed even when I had to pretend I did not."

DREAMS OF YOUTH

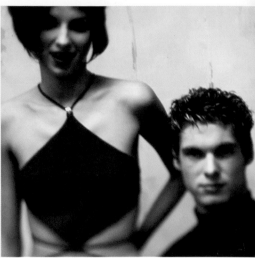

ABOVE Dreaming of puberty might mean that we are working through crucial life changes in our dreams.

ABOVE RIGHT Adolescent and teenage years can represent rebellion and flux, and if we dream of this stage it may be that in our waking lives we are trying to find the right course of action to take.

YOUTH IS A TIME WHEN WE THROW OFF BOTH THE CONSTRAINTS AND THE INNOCENCE OF CHILDHOOD, TESTING AUTHORITY FIGURES AND TRYING TO FIND OUR OWN WAY IN LIFE. IN OUR TEENAGE YEARS WE EXPERIENCE THE PHYSICAL CHANGES OF PUBERTY, DISCOVER OUR SEXUALITY, HANG OUT IN GANGS, SUFFER FROM INTENSE PEER PRESSURE, AND DISCOVER OUR POWER AS YOUNG ADULTS. BUT OUR OWN EXPERIENCE AS TEENAGERS — GOOD AND BAD — WILL BE REFLECTED IN OUR DREAMS AS MUCH AS THE STEREOTYPES OF THIS LIFE STAGE, SO DREAMS OF YOUTH WILL MEAN VERY DIFFERENT THINGS TO DIFFERENT PEOPLE.

GROWING PAINS

Many people find adolescence to be a tumultuous and painful period, and some of us carry the scars for the rest of our lives. It is a time of transition from childhood to adulthood, and indeed the key take-home message of dreams about adolescence may well be metamorphosis. At this age we are not yet used to the changes in our bodies, and also often feel awkward and embarrassed at the errors we make in our quest to seem grown-up. To make things worse, we may be teased for the very mistakes we make and the changes we are going through, and withdraw as a result. Dreaming of youth later in life may mean that we are going through changes about which we feel uncertain or unconfident. We may be anticipating criticism or ridicule, or even fear that we will not be taken seriously by society. Even if your dream doesn't actually give you answers or guidance, it should be a useful way of making you aware of how you feel about the changes and what your fears are.

PEER GROUP

At the same time as we begin to rebel against the adult world and leave our childhood ways behind, we turn instead to our peers, with whom we can identify more strongly, for ideas, support and encouragement as much as

RIGHT The desire to be part of the "in-crowd" is probably at its most intense during youth, so if you dream about this it might reflect a feeling you have of being on the edge of things, of being not quite accepted.

friendship. Because the peer group becomes so important, many teenagers feel the need to conform – to adopt current fashions, have the latest gear, and even to use the right words, in order to be acceptable. In our youth we are testing out new roles, so there may be a lot of faking involved in our behaviour before we become settled in who we are. For this reason, dreams of adolescence may also be about inauthenticity, about following trends or trying to find a niche within an accepted set.

EXTREMES AND IDEALS

Because we have so many new experiences as teenagers and young adults, this period of our lives may seem to be one of extremes, especially in our feelings and behaviours. We may be more passionately in love at this time than at any other later time in our lives, or be filled with despair when things don't go our way. It is a time when we are most likely to feel prepared to step into the unknown, travel the world on a shoestring or take up dangerous sports. This is when we are at our physical peak, and feel able to do all these things because we have a sense of being invincible, immortal. It is also a time of pushing the boundaries – partying all night long, getting very drunk or experimenting with drugs – and exploring social or political ideals. We may still do all these things or have the same feelings later in life, but as a stereotype, we are more likely to associate them with being young, and youth may be the theme of our dream to represent our desire to try new things, to step back from the mundane practicalities of life and remind ourselves of our own ideals.

LOOKING AHEAD

In our youthful explorations of the big wide world, we are in the process of finding where we belong in society and what we want to do with our lives. We leave school and have to make choices about work or further education, and begin to assert our own personal style and beliefs. While dreams about youth may be about immaturity in yourself or others, they could also be about discovering and asserting yourself.

NOSTALGIA

Looking back at our youth, we may feel nostalgic, remembering the freedom, the fun, the passion and excitement, and forgetting the more painful moments. We may even be reconstructing a youth that we never really had, perhaps one that seems more fun and interesting than our own. If we are afraid of growing old, we may be rejecting the stereotypes of middle or old age and clinging to youthfulness, rather than embracing the positive aspects our current stage of life can offer.

ABOVE If you dream of a lack of financial freedom in youth perhaps you are admitting to a feeling that this has never really gone away, and that this is materially a real problem for you.
ABOVE LEFT The excitement and intensity of your first romance can never be matched. If you dream of young love perhaps it reflects a dissatisfaction with your love life.
ABOVE FAR LEFT Dreaming of the wilder side of youth culture might mean that you are yearning for a more exciting element in your life, whatever your age.

DREAM OF YOUTH

"In my dream I had dyed my hair red and wore a biker's jacket, and I was behaving like a teenager again. Not that I dyed my hair when I was a teenager, but in my dream it made me feel young again. Since I passed forty I've got it into my head that I must be wild, rebellious and wacky to recapture my youth and ward off middle age and all the implications of sedateness that that time of life has. I think I'm also a little jealous of my own teenage children and the fun they seem to have."

THE MIDDLE YEARS

THE PREOCCUPATIONS OF OUR MIDDLE YEARS TEND TO BE MORE PRAGMATIC THAN THOSE OF OUR ADOLESCENCE – WORK, PARTNERS, CHILDREN AND PROPERTY ARE LIKELY TO DOMINATE OUR THOUGHTS. IT IS ALSO A TIME WHEN WE COME INTO OUR OWN AS ADULTS – BECOMING ESTABLISHED IN VARIOUS WAYS, TAKING ON RESPONSIBILITIES AND MAKING DECISIONS AND JUDGEMENTS BASED ON EXPERIENCE RATHER THAN CONJECTURE. AT THE SAME TIME, WE MAY REGRET THE LOSS OF YOUTHFUL FREEDOM AND STRENGTH OR FEAR THE APPROACH OF OLD AGE. WHATEVER AGE WE ARE THERE WILL BE HAPPIER TIMES, WORSE TIMES, AND WE WILL LOOK BACK WITH REGRET OR FONDNESS. IN OUR DREAMS THIS MAY BE INTENSIFIED.

THE MATERIAL WORLD

As adults we often define ourselves by the job we have or the work we do, and others also judge us and position us in the social hierarchy accordingly. Our self-esteem may be bolstered or dented by the status of our job, or by not having any work. Changing careers can be a difficult time as we adjust our self-image, perhaps getting used to being on the bottom rung of a different career ladder.

Work also brings money, and with it the many benefits and encumbrances of the material world. In particular, buying our first property is a material milestone, with the implications of commitment to staying put and to being able to finance the purchase for years to come. Living in our own home also gives us the opportunity to express our personal style in the type of home we buy and in how we furnish it.

Our relationship with material things may be an aesthetic statement, and it may be about making life easier or more enjoyable, but it is often also about status and power.

Dreaming of acquiring something may be wish fulfilment around a particular object, or it could be that you want a change of lifestyle which that object represents. If it is higher social standing you are after, this could be related to your sense of self-worth rather than external issues. We also become attached to things and worry about losing them, or about being tied down by our possessions, and this may manifest itself in our dreams.

SETTLING DOWN

As well as becoming materially established and leaving youth behind, we may start actively looking for a partner, someone with whom we might settle down and perhaps start a family. But while some people feel their lives will be meaningless or unbearably insecure without these things, the idea of "settling down" may fill others with horror and they may prefer the kind of freedom that is only possible without such ties. Such preferences will influence how you read dreams in which these aspects of adulthood are significant. Dreams of "settling down" may be a form of wish fulfilment, or a way of trying out a different lifestyle. In a less literal sense though, they could indicate a sense of being settled

BELOW All of our rites of passage will become food for our dreams but probably none will be more intense than our first real love, as we move in together, set up home and start to plan a family.

in yourself and knowing what you want – even if your lifestyle doesn't seem to reflect this – or a desire for stability.

MIDDLE AGE

The stereotype of middle age that we may use symbolically in our dreams is likely to be one of settled routine and staidness. However, it can also be a time of great change and readjustment as roles alter, and these aspects may figure in a person's dreams at this time. After years of striving to establish ourselves, we may feel at a loss as to how to proceed once this is achieved. The midlife crisis that many people go through is prompted by the vision of life developing into routine. Dreams can hint at other possibilities or make us aware of exactly what is bothering us about our circumstances.

EXPERIENCE

Whatever path your life takes, the experience you gain on the way can give you maturity and insight, and it may be this aspect of adulthood that is being reflected in your dreams rather than specific rites of passage.

Although our physical form and strength gradually declines over the years, we may feel increasingly confident in ourselves and in what we do. We may come to have authority and power over others and take on increasing responsibilities. Our dreams can be a useful vehicle for coming to terms with this, and with the relationship they put us in towards others, and how we learn to handle them.

ABOVE We put our mark on our home as soon as we move in and we may well dream about it as we adapt to the newness of it all.
LEFT Dreaming of moving house might be indicative of some other kind of change in our life that we need to cope with.
BELOW Dreams of children could indicate a readiness to take on the major responsibilities of being a parent.

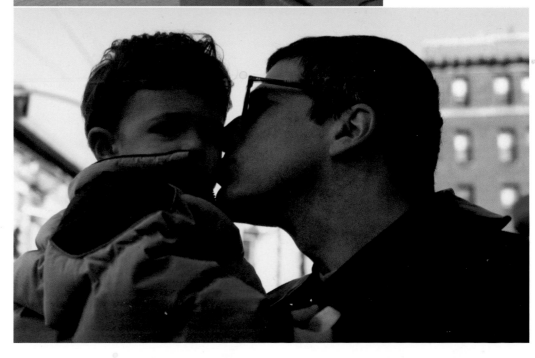

AGEING

WE ARE GETTING OLDER ALL THE TIME, AND GRADUALLY THE FEAR OF WHAT THIS MEANS FOR US AND OF WHAT COMES NEXT BEGINS TO PERMEATE OUR UNCONSCIOUS AND WORK ON OUR IMAGINATION. WE KNOW OR FEAR THE HORRORS OF THE FIRST GREY HAIRS, OF WRINKLES AND AN EXPANDING WAISTLINE. WE ARE AWARE THAT WE MIGHT BECOME INFIRM OR ILL, OR LOSE OUR MENTAL FACULTIES WHEN WE GROW OLD. BUT THESE FEARS CAN ALSO BE BALANCED BY THE WISDOM THAT A LIFETIME'S EXPERIENCE MAY HAVE BROUGHT US, AND OLD AGE CAN BE A TIME WHEN WE ALLOW OURSELVES TO ATTAIN A LEVEL OF PEACE AND CONTEMPLATION.

We dream of ageing for several reasons. It may be that we are worried about it, about losing our youthful looks and our physical strength and ability. It could also be that we are coming to terms with ageing, content with what we have seen and done so far in our lives and looking forward to the prospect of a comfortable and interesting retirement. A dream of old age may also be a metaphor for times past, and serve as a kind of nostalgia trip.

FEARS OF AGEING

We all react to the fear of growing old in different ways. We may face up to it, but often this is too painful and we choose instead to deny the unpleasant realities of old age, or to suppress them by ignoring them or laughing them off. We try to reverse the ageing process by going for cosmetic surgery, dyeing our hair, applying anti-ageing creams, and wearing youthful clothes.

Our unconscious is not easily deceived though, and will deal with our fears in our dreams if we don't do so in our waking lives. It knows that we are terrified at the prospect of our lives ending and our bodies decaying, that we are afraid to confront the possibility that when we reach old age and drop the frantic activity of our younger years, we will discover that it has all been meaningless.

Dreams in which we see ourselves getting older, or already old, can be quite shocking, and act as a wake-up call for us to pay more attention to what we are doing with our lives, to make us realise that time is passing. Sometimes these dreams mask a concern about our health, and may be taken as a cautionary note to make sure we remain as fit and active as we ought to. Recurring dreams about ageing may indicate an ongoing concern, and if you have them it is important to get to the bottom of what is bothering you.

RETIRING

Even if you are still fit and active, retiring from the working world can be the first step in starting to acknowledge that old age is not far off. You may dream about retirement in a literal way if you are approaching it in your own life, or if your partner or parents are soon to retire. This will provide you with a way to

BELOW RIGHT As time passes we can start to feel edgy, as if there are things to do that we need to concentrate on.
BELOW How we feel about our health will be shadowed in our dreams – if we are healthy while asleep it is pretty much how we will feel when we are awake.

A DREAM OF AGEING

"I was looking in a mirror and while I watched I saw my own teeth fall out and my hair turn white. The whole ageing process was immensely speeded up. I know I am getting older, but this dream really shocked me and made me feel that I wanted to hang on to my youth at all costs. But it also made me realize that I really have to enjoy what I've got because time goes so fast and I won't have it for long. And as it all slips away I have to keep reminding myself to enjoy each and every moment."

LEFT As we get older we do get more experienced, better equipped to be successful. If our dreams reflect this we can be reassured about how we fit in to the world around us.

explore possible anxieties you have around this transition.

How you see retirement will depend to a considerable extent on how well you are prepared for it, both financially and emotionally. It can be difficult to adjust to the lack of structure and activity, the loss of status, the lack of contact with your colleagues, and the sheer weight of idle time that you now have. But you may equally see it as a time to reap the benefits of your hard work, to enjoy a leisurely life or turn your hand to hobbies or other interests you have not had time for before.

WITHDRAWAL

Whatever your age, your dreams may also use retirement or old age as a metaphor for withdrawing – especially from society or from an overly active lifestyle. Indeed old age is for many a time when our contact with the outside world lessens as our ability or desire to get out decreases and our friends and siblings die. It can be a lonely time, and it may be this that your dream is trying to draw to your attention – either your own fear of becoming isolated, or guilt at not paying enough attention to an elderly relative.

WISDOM

Our stereotypes of old age are not all negative though, and while the elderly are often marginalized in Western society, we may find the archetypal figure of the wise old man or woman appearing in our dreams as a source of advice or understanding; we may even be that figure ourselves.

Grandparents or other familiar old faces may also crop up in our dreams as symbols of stability and continuity, allowing us to feel grounded and supported in our family, and giving us perspective on our lives.

BELOW FAR LEFT To dream of old or worn-out objects might point to something in our life that we feel needs to be rejuvenated.
BELOW LEFT Dreaming of possible loneliness in old age might reflect the way you feel about your life currently rather than a fear of the future.
BELOW But even when there is no hope of living forever we can rest assured that there is new life even in our dreams.

DEATH

WE ALL KNOW THAT SOONER OR LATER, DEATH WILL COME TO US, HOPEFULLY NOT PREMATURELY, BUT AS THE INEVITABLE AND INESCAPABLE LAST STAGE IN THE CYCLE OF LIFE. HOWEVER MUCH WE TRY TO AVOID THINKING ABOUT OUR OWN DEATH, OR THAT OF OUR LOVED ONES, OUR UNCONSCIOUS WILL AT SOME STAGE START TO ADDRESS THE ISSUE AND TRY TO PREPARE US FOR IT. THERE ARE MANY ISSUES ASSOCIATED WITH DEATH THAT MIGHT FEATURE IN OUR DREAMS: LOSS, LONELINESS OR RELEASE FOR EXAMPLE, AND WHETHER OR NOT THERE IS LIFE AFTER DEATH MIGHT BE ANOTHER THEME THAT WE MAY TRY TO SPECULATE ON AND EXPLORE IN OUR DREAMS.

COMING TO TERMS WITH MORTALITY

Dreams of funerals or graveyards, grief and mourning, dead bodies or skeletons may be quite literally about death and dying, and often show that we view this process in a negative light. If we are worried about death and dying then dreams of death probably happen to make us do something to try to come to terms with our own mortality. But if we dream of people celebrating, being happy, remembering the dead person with pride and love, then perhaps we have made some progress in coming to terms with it. This doesn't necessarily mean we have to look forward to it, but merely that it holds no power over us to frighten us, and that we are as prepared as we can be for this event.

A LOVED ONE'S DEATH

Dreams about others dying may indicate a worry that they will die or leave us. Who we dream about may be telling us who we most fear will leave us, but it could also be that rather than a literal death, the dream represents some figurative termination of a quality that you particularly value (or dislike) in that person.

IMAGES OF DEATH

History has given us many morbid death images which our society seems to have taken eagerly on board – vaults and misty graveyards, mourners dressed in black, skeletons and gravediggers, crows, the Grim Reaper, and countless images of hell. People down the ages seem to have enjoyed frightening and torturing themselves with such images, and in your dreams they could point to disturbance and fear around death. Dreaming of being buried – especially being buried alive – may have nothing to do with death but rather a feeling of having the life squeezed out of you, of being stifled in some way.

But death is not always disturbing – it can be very undramatic, even mundane, or very peaceful and part of the natural order. A graveyard in your dream may be a beautiful, calm place where you spend time remembering people you loved.

LIFE AFTER DEATH

Death is our biggest rite of passage, the one that takes us out of this existence and on into the next – whatever that might be. If we do believe that death is merely a transition into the next life, our unconscious may choose to show us images of change, of journeys and rebirth – which may indicate that it knows that death is not final but is indeed merely a symptom of great transformation. These dreams may be suggesting radical change or the need for such change, and not actual physical death.

How we dream about death reflects not only our views of the process but also our views of what we think happens to us afterwards. We may dream of heaven or hell as if we know what they are like, though such imagery is generally based on

BELOW Even if we never consciously think about our mortality it will be a source of worry to us on a deep level. We might also dream of death as a way of focusing on worries that we have of being separated from others.

LEFT Images of death don't have to be negative. They can also generate a feeling of ultimate peace and tranquillity that we may feel we need.

BELOW The religious trappings of death might suggest an awful state of nothingness, or inspire awe and acceptance. It depends on how we view death.

countless images that have been handed down to us by others. Such dreams may indicate some kind of self-judgement, seeking reward for good behaviour or fearing punishment for bad.

Whatever else it may involve, death means separation from the body, so may reveal a wish for release from ill health. It could also mean that we are coming to terms with our preoccupations with the body, or, less literally, the material world.

ABOVE Standard images of death in our dreams might actually be about some other kind of rite of passage, and perhaps something quite mundane in comparison.

LEFT Whatever religion we follow will give us plenty of imagery to fuel our dreams and visions of death and the afterworld.
RIGHT Dreaming of someone's death might mean you are reflecting on the passing of a relationship, or a phase of your friendship together.

DREAM OF DEATH

"I was in a foreign country like Egypt, being buried alive. I could feel the sand filling my mouth and my body sinking deeper and deeper into the ground. I felt I was suffocating. Just then someone uncovered my face with a spade and I could breathe. They said, 'look – some bones!' and I realized I had been dead for a long time.

I think the whole dream was about an inability to change. I felt it meant that I had to look at what was important to me, and get rid of a lot of things in my life so that I was not so stuck and held back by my possessions and rigid attitudes. I think there was also a fear that it might actually be too late to change."

MIND, BODY AND SPIRIT

Our emotional and physical experiences, together with the things we are told or learn throughout our lives, give us a framework for our beliefs, which we try, often unsuccessfully, to use to keep us safe in times of trouble and crisis. With experience we have the opportunity to develop an understanding of our limitations, to grow and change, learn and expand. Some say that through such experiences our soul also learns and grows; when we have learnt all we need to, we move on. At times these lessons are enjoyable, but often we learn best through adversity. We incorporate our experiences, our hopes and our fears into our dreams. It is here that our unconscious tries to come to terms with guilt or with the heartache of grief; explores our sexuality and faces our mortality; and endeavours to answer some of the great questions of our existence.

EMOTIONS

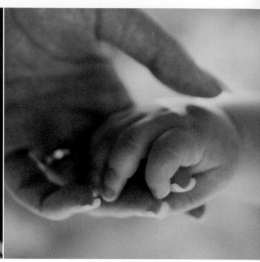

ABOVE Sometimes we are not aware that we feel angry or frustrated, but such feelings can surface in our dreams.
ABOVE RIGHT Our dream symbolism may indicate painful emotions. This image could suggest isolation and loneliness.
ABOVE FAR RIGHT Holding a baby's hand is a symbol of love and tenderness. It may also mean a need to protect or be protected.

OUR EMOTIONS COVER A VAST RANGE OF EXPERIENCES, FROM ANGER AND JEALOUSY THROUGH BOREDOM AND SADNESS TO LOVE AND HAPPINESS. WHILE WE ARE ONLY TOO GLAD TO HAVE THE POSITIVE EMOTIONS, OTHERS ARE UNCOMFORTABLE AND WE MAY TRY TO PUSH THEM AWAY. BUT WE CAN'T ALWAYS CONTROL THEM, AND THEY CAN WELL UP AND OVERWHELM US, TAKING US BY SURPRISE. IN OUR DREAMS WE EXPERIENCE THE FULL RANGE OF OUR EMOTIONS, OFTEN MORE INTENSELY THAN IN OUR WAKING LIVES, AND THEY MAY HELP US COME TO GRIPS WITH THE REALLY DIFFICULT ONES.

BURIED EMOTIONS
We often hide or lose track of our emotions because we want to appear mature or civilized or in control. At times strong emotions threaten to take us over and then we may be afraid of seeming weak or vulnerable, or of doing something that we will later regret, or simply of wasting time that we think we should be spending on something else. We develop coping mechanisms to make sure that our feelings don't show, and some people are so successful at this that they lose touch with their feelings. They may also divert attention from one emotion and express it as another that may seem more

socially acceptable – for instance, men who have been brought up to believe that "boys don't cry" may express sadness as anger, and conversely many women who have had their anger curbed by social or parental disapproval may cry when angry.

When we control or divert our emotions we may delude ourselves into feeling stronger, braver, wiser, or in some other way more acceptable, but there is often a price to pay for being cut off in this way. We need to feel and express our true emotions if we are to be well-rounded and complete human beings, to find a balance between heart and mind. Our dreams can

help us to do this by unlocking unacknowledged feelings.

FEELINGS IN DREAMS
It is always worth looking at the feelings that come up in a dream. Usually they are consistent with what you would imagine you should be feeling in the context of the dream, but sometimes the feelings and the plot may be puzzlingly at odds. Events may occur in your dream precisely to provoke a response that you will take note of, to make you think about what is really going on inside you. Sometimes this can be hard – if you always play the role of the kind and loving mother, for instance, a dream in

Dreaming permits each and every one of us to be quietly and safely insane every night of our lives.
WILLIAM DEMENT

which you sit reading a book impassively while your children are tormented will be really shocking and hard to come to terms with, but it could be a reality check on your ability to be the saint all the time, and may bring to your attention your frustrations or the fact that your own needs are not being met.

EMOTIONAL POINTERS

In some dreams the emotional content will be the take-home message rather than any events or images, and it may even be that the only thing you remember about the dream is that it was terrifying, or that in it you were extremely anxious about running out of time.

If you are not ready to deal with emotions square on, though, your mind may produce symbols to stand in for these feelings. Virtually all of your dream images can be read symbolically, or are present in your dream because they provoke some strong emotion or train of thought. Some are fairly obvious – for example a heart may stand for romantic love – while others are less clear but nevertheless widely accepted – such as the notion that water in all its many forms represents our emotions. Many of the symbols we use to represent emotions are discussed more fully elsewhere.

The main thing is to look at the context of the symbol and your response to it in order to be able to access the emotional content. Once you understand what emotions are being brought to the surface and how they come across in your dream, you will probably have a clearer idea of how to deal with them in a useful and positive way.

ABOVE Expressing strong emotions can have a knock-on effect in our dealings with others.
ABOVE LEFT Dream imagery is often bizarre. Feeling tied-up in knots is frustrating and can make you feel like screaming.
ABOVE FAR LEFT Emotions that are held back or suppressed in your waking life may surface later in your dreams.

LEFT To dream of a macho man may suggest that it is hard for you to own your feelings as you like to appear "cool".
FAR LEFT The context of our dreams is important. A mother with her baby will mean different things for each of us, depending on our circumstances.

LOSS AND GRIEF

WHEN DEATH ENTERS OUR LIVES IT OFTEN COMES AS A COMPLETE SHOCK, AND WE ARE LEFT BEWILDERED, LOST, ANGRY AND CONFUSED. ADDED TO THE PAIN ARE FEELINGS OF REGRET AND GUILT, THE SENSE OF "IF ONLY I'D KNOWN", "IF ONLY I'D BEEN ABLE TO SAY ALL THE THINGS I WANTED TO", OR "I DIDN'T GET A CHANCE TO SAY GOODBYE". BUT IT ISN'T JUST DEATH THAT GENERATES FEELINGS OF LOSS. DIVORCE, REDUNDANCY AND EVEN THE LOSS OF PRIZED POSSESSIONS CAN BRING THEIR OWN SUDDEN SHOCKS TO OUR LIFE. HOW WE COPE CAN AFFECT HOW MUCH FINDS ITS WAY INTO OUR DREAMS, AND IT IS HERE THAT WE WILL TRY TO COME TO TERMS WITH THIS LOSS IF WE ARE NOT FACING UP TO IT IN OUR WAKING LIFE.

GRIEVING

The word "bereaved" is from an Old English word *bereafian*, which means "to plunder". And that is the feeling we have when we have lost someone or something close to us. We feel plundered, we feel that someone or something precious has been carried off without our permission or knowledge.

The experience of bereavement is not only triggered by a person's death, but other significant life events, such as divorce, separation and redundancy. The loss of such things as our health or our youth – or even our personal possessions – also have associations with grief and loss, and may affect us quite deeply.

Whatever the reason for our grief, we may try to work it out in our dreams. A lot of people are shocked and surprised if grieving continues in their dreams when they think they have "got over it", but the stronger the emotional tie, the longer the process is likely to go on. After someone you were close to has died, they may return to your dreams from time to time for the rest of your life.

ABOVE Although we may chide ourselves for being silly, the loss of a precious possession is likely to stir up our emotions. If you dream of your lost treasure, consider what it symbolizes for you.

FUNERALS

A funeral is an official ending. It gives us a chance to say "goodbye" and to mourn our loss. In some cultures, open displays of crying and even wailing are perfectly natural at funerals, and grieving can be expected to last, and be marked with cermonies, for months. In western society we are expected to "pull ourselves together" or "put on a brave face" and get on with our lives as quickly as possible, and far too little time or emotional energy is given to grieving. Yet if we have not fully come to terms with someone's death, they will in a sense, haunt us. Once there has been a proper grieving process, our dreams will by and large return to normal.

BELOW It is very common when someone close to us dies that they continue to appear in our dreams – for months, or even years afterwards. This may be to help us work out aspects of our relationship with that person.

WORKING IT OUT

In our dreams the person or object we have lost may appear in glorious technicolour. They may seem perfectly normal and present, just as they were in life, and on waking we may feel the shock and sadness all over again when we realize it was "just a dream". This process is essential to our unconscious even if it is difficult and confusing for us. To our unconscious it is a way of working out what has happened and laying the ghost to rest. It also gives us the opportunity to say things that we feel were left unsaid, or to replay events in our unconscious mind so that we can be with our loved one once more. It is a hard and sometimes wrenching process but essential if we are to be able to get on with our lives and become as whole and as healed as possible.

DREAMS OF LOSS

Losing things in a dream may indicate that you need to mourn a loss or achieve closure on some aspect of your life. It may be something physical, such as a valuable object, or it could be more abstract, such as the loss of freedom, or of a particular phase in your life that has ended – for instance the transition from being single to being married. Even something frivolous, like having your hair cut, can be traumatic if it represents a loss of identity.

In all these cases there is a period of adjustment as you come to terms with losing something that is integral to your self-expression, or that reminds you of someone you love.

LEFT There is no easy way to mourn, but spending quiet time alone each day in reflection can help you come to terms with your loss.

MIDDLE LEFT A graveyard appearing in your dreams could be a reminder to lay the past to rest and move on with your life.

BOTTOM LEFT Piles of money in a dream may represent concerns with material security. What do you fear to lose?

GRIEF DREAM

"The year that my grandmother died I saw her in my dreams every night for months. Every morning when I woke up, I was convinced she was still alive and would run into my parents' room to tell them the good news; every morning they had to tell me she was dead. I felt the shock anew each time. It was terrible and sad, and for a good while I was frightened to go to sleep at night because I didn't want to face the shock in the morning. I even left notes to myself by my bed saying 'Granny is dead'. Each morning I woke grieving the loss. I think it helped. I feel that I can talk about her now and remember her with warmth and love."

GUILT AND BLAME

MANY PEOPLE ARE SURPRISED TO ENCOUNTER GUILT AND BLAME IN THEIR DREAMS, BUT THEY ARE AMONG THE COMMONEST OF DREAM THEMES AND PERMEATE BOTH OUR LIVES AND OUR DREAMS ON MANY LEVELS. WE MAY THINK THAT A DREAM IN WHICH WE ARE A CONVICT OR AN ADULTERER IS JUST OUR UNCONSCIOUS EXPLORING FACETS OF OUR CHARACTER THAT WE MIGHT NOT LIKE TO OWN UP TO IN OUR WAKING LIFE, BUT IT IS OFTEN GUILT THAT OUR UNCONSCIOUS IS EXPLORING. EVEN IF WE SEEM TO BE DREAMING SOMEONE ELSE'S GUILT OR BLAMING SOMEONE FOR SOMETHING, IT MAY WELL BE A DISPLACED REPRESENTATION OF OUR OWN GUILT AND SELF-BLAME.

FEELING GUILTY

Our conscious minds are very experienced at justifying our actions or blaming others so that we avoid uncomfortable feelings of guilt and self-blame. If we know we have been cruel or difficult to someone, or mishandled another person in some way, the unconscious may try to make us more aware of our behaviour so that we can see what we have done. For deep down we know what is right and wrong, and we know that we need to understand the implications of our actions and make amends for them. Part of the role of the unconscious in our dreams is to drive us towards a greater self-awareness and understanding.

Even people who are by and large decent and honest will have the occasional lapse, and may feel disproportionately guilty and remorseful as a result. Our guilt may be misplaced too; children are often punished for being angry, and as they grow up, and even into adulthood they may continue to feel guilty when they feel anger. Adults who have this kind of problem with anger may also carry a subconscious fear of retribution as a result of anger.

CRIME AND PUNISHMENT

The greater the offence, the more intense the dream is likely to be, and we may wake feeling we have actually committed a crime, even if whatever is making us feel guilty is not the same as the dream scenario. The nature of the offence in our dream will usually give us enough clues to identify what it is we are feeling guilty about. It may be that you are being caught – or simply blamed – for a wrongdoing and you feel guilty until proven innocent. Take note of whether the punishment fits the crime – if you are given a hefty penalty for a mere peccadillo, it may be that you are feeling victimized by injustice rather than actually feeling guilty.

CONFESSION

Confessing in a dream, whether to a priest, a confidante or to the person you have wronged, also indicates that you feel guilty for something. It may also show that you are trying to purge yourself of your guilty feelings and regrets, or offload the burden of guilt on to someone else.

We treat ourselves badly at times and we may feel compelled to double the damage by "beating ourselves up" about it. Such guilt and self-blame may manifest as

BELOW Sometimes our inner voice must shout to be heard and can be symbolized in our dreams as threatening, or aggressive figures. Ask yourself what it is that you don't want to hear. Maybe you have a fear of being punished?

LEFT Fragments of our dreams are often all that we recall, but only you can decide if they make you feel guilty.

LEFT To be standing accused in your dream may tie-in with harbouring a guilty secret. Who is it that you are wronging and what is it that you fear from them?

dreams about being punished. It doesn't have to be crimes that we feel guilty for. Sometimes we feel bad about withholding love, or for not responding to someone's distress, or for failing to rise to a challenge. We may even feel guilty whenever we please ourselves rather than pleasing someone else and judge ourselves "selfish".

Guilt is one of those insidious feelings that seem to spill into every area of our lives. It has the power to go on eating away at us forever and it is often extremely hard to get rid of. But our dreams may give us a clue as to what we can do to work through such feelings, and learn from them. Ask questions of your dream and the answers will emerge.

ABOVE Feeling guilty and being a victim often go hand-in-hand. Who or what would you like to turn your back on?

DREAM OF BLAME

"I was riding a motorbike and saw my son riding towards me. We both pulled back on our handlebars and did 'wheelies'. The strange thing is my son is only five but in my dream he was a young man. I feel really guilty towards him because his mother and I separated. Even though it was his mother that left, I still feel so much of his pain at not having her there, at having to grow up ahead of his time. I feel responsible for this because I must have played a part in her decision to leave."

ABOVE To dream of a prison cell may symbolize being punished for some misdemeanour. Could it be your guilt that has imprisoned you?

RIGHT Our guilt can make us feel small and trapped. It can remind us of how it felt as children to be accused of a crime we didn't commit.

FALLING IN LOVE

MORE SONGS, POEMS AND LETTERS HAVE BEEN WRITTEN ABOUT LOVE THAN ANY OTHER SUBJECT, AND IT IS ONLY NATURAL THAT SUCH AN IMPORTANT EMOTION SHOULD FIGURE SO LARGELY IN OUR DREAMS. WE ALL NEED TO LOVE AND BE LOVED, AND WHEN WE FALL IN LOVE WE LITERALLY CAN'T STOP DAYDREAMING ABOUT OUR CHOSEN ONE, SO IT IS COMPLETELY UNDERSTANDABLE THAT THIS CARRIES ON INTO OUR SLEEPING WORLDS TOO. FALLING IN LOVE AND HOLDING THE STEADY LOVE OF A REAL PERSON ARE TWO DIFFERENT THINGS, BUT BOTH REPRESENT OR CONTAIN POWERFUL EMOTIONS, AND MAY DOMINATE OUR DREAMS FROM TIME TO TIME.

In our dreams our partner may take on a new dimension – not who they really are but who we think they are, or who we would like them to be. They may be wilder, fiercer, bossier, kinder, more or less loving, but their essence remains the same. Our unconscious may amplify an aspect of their character to draw our attention to some particular point of view so we can adjust our relationship accordingly, or in order to flag up characteristics that we don't want to see.

FIRST LOVE

For teenagers, falling in love is often a painful experience. Our first love affair can be very formative, as all our future relationships may be built on the lessons we learn in those first few soulful gazes or fumbling embraces. Likewise, that first ever love affair will probably feature prominently in our teen dreams.

It is also quite natural, especially at this young age, to fall in love with someone who is unattainable – someone we adore from afar, or who is forbidden – perhaps because they are too old for us, or are already in a partnership. This person is likely to appear in our dreams, which may have a sexual or erotic bias. Such dreams can be very realistic and make us feel confused and embarrassed, particularly when we meet the person in daily life.

ROMANCE

A kind of scene-setting for love, romance usually features more prominently at the beginning of a relationship when our feelings are based more in fantasy than in the reality of the person on whom we have focused our attentions. At this stage it functions as wish fulfilment – we want everything to be wonderful and so we put all our effort into impressing the other person and making them feel special. We also want to be made to feel special ourselves. Romance provides a smoke screen, a context and loose set of rules and rituals in the framework of which we can get to know the other person, but it may also serve to distract us from who they really are.

The symbols and activities that we associate with romance – anything heart-shaped, candlelit dinners, sunsets on the beach, love poetry and so on – are many and wide-ranging, so dreaming of these things, whether they

BELOW RIGHT When we are in love, it can feel as if we are floating on air and our dreams may have a romantic feel to them. **BELOW** Falling in love is an exciting experience and it is most likely that our lover will keep on appearing in our dreams.

involve a particular person or not, may point to a wish for romance in our lives or the possibility that it is on the horizon. Men in particular may find themselves feeling particularly vulnerable if they show their softer side, so a romantic dream may have more to do with getting in touch with vulnerability and owning your feelings than with any kind of actual partnership.

Whether the romantic dream scenario will hold together coherently or is flawed in some way may also be taken as a hint as to how you should be approaching love and relationships. Ask yourself whether you are looking for a person to have a real relationship with or merely someone who will make you feel better by distracting you from areas of dissatisfaction in your life.

THE FOOD OF LOVE

Love and food go together in many ways, so you could consider whether food images in your dreams are linked to love. For many people food and drink are an intrinsic part of the rituals of romance and courtship, and are also the subject of fetishes. Your unconscious may make reference to expressions such as "all-consuming passion" when it dreams of eating, to suggest the nature of how you relate to a lover, and perhaps to warn you not to become too obsessive.

DREAM OF LOVE

"I was madly in love with my girlfriend's mother and dreamed of her every night for months. Every morning I would walk my girlfriend to school. Her mother would see her off, and I would barely be able to talk to her. In fact I only really went out with the daughter so I could see the mother every morning. The dreams were all quite erotic, although we never made love either in my dream or in real life. There was no way I could ever have had a relationship with her in reality for lots of different reasons, so this was my substitute."

SEX

The master of the erotic dream is undoubtedly Freud, who held that much of what we dream, even if it seems to have absolutely nothing to do with sex, symbolizes suppressed sexual desires. In the Freudian model, a snake, ladder, knife, staircase, candle or pen represent the penis, and caves, boxes, tunnels or dark rooms are the vagina. But while it is possible that such objects may act as symbols in this way, they are not necessarily doing so in every case, and as previously discussed, symbols will have different meanings for different people. We may also work with our sexuality directly through overtly erotic dreams.

ABOVE Erotic and stylized images may appear in our dreams, but only you will understand how they relate to you.
ABOVE RIGHT The kinds of things you dream about might be symbolically, or overtly sexual.
ABOVE FAR RIGHT For both men and women, snakes are a traditional symbol of sexual power and energy. Are you comfortable with your sexuality?

Many dreams contain symbolism that only you will understand. Certain things may have become associated with sex for you by dint of your experiences – for example, if there was music playing the first time you made love, the same tune may always trigger the memory of your first sexual experience.

SEXUAL FANTASIES

Two common sexual fantasies are of having sex in a public place and having sex with a stranger. Such dreams will tend to have different meanings for men and women because their basic sexual needs and responses differ.

Dreaming of making love in a crowded stadium, for instance, may reflect the tendency of men to boast about sex, or a woman's desire to be less inhibited. In this kind of dream a woman may be showing a need to be cheered on or encouraged by others to express her sexuality in a full and satisfying way, or she may enjoy the fact that she is capable of doing so and wants to let the world know about it.

If the dream is of having sex in a lift or on public transport, it may highlight the fun and thrilling aspect to sex, and remind us how it feels to do something "naughty". Such a dream may bring into question your attitude to rules and social behaviour and may show a desire to break a taboo.

For men, the biological imperative to spread their seed widely is met with confusingly divergent attitudes in society – on the one hand it is frowned on as infidelity and on the other it is prized as prowess. So dreams of sex with a stranger may reveal a yearning for just this model of

People don't fall in love with what's right in front of them. People want the dream – what they can't have. The more unattainable, the more attractive.

XANDER

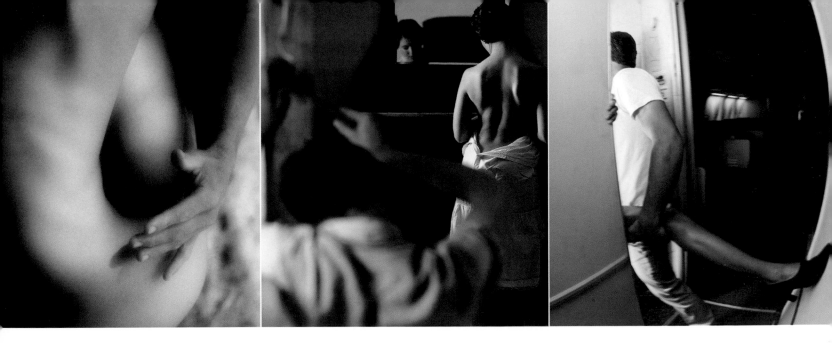

behaviour, either to escape social restrictions and enjoy the taste of forbidden fruit, or to reassure the man of his virility.

WISH FULFILMENT

Your sexual desires and urges do not simply go away if you are on your own, and you will probably find other ways to express them. The more cut off you are from a healthy sex life, the more likely it is that sex will appear in your dreams as a substitute for the real thing. If there is no-one special in your life you may dream of sex with a stranger, or perhaps you have met someone you desire and can't wait to be intimate with in real life. Even if you have a relationship, you may be expressing your desire for something better if your present situation is unsatisfactory. Whatever the case, these dreams are usually healthy explorations of possibilities or expressions of our needs, and we can use them as a guide to how we are feeling.

SEXUAL PROBLEMS

We may have erotic dreams that help us deal with our sexual difficulties. Our problems could be quite obvious – for example frustration at not having a sexual partner – or your unconscious might be drawing to your attention something you haven't even admitted to yourself yet. Even if you feel unable to talk about a problem, you will still need to process it and try to overcome it or come to terms with it, and your dreams can provide a useful framework for doing just this.

DISCOVERING OUR SEXUALITY

Adolescence is a time of sexual discovery and exploration, but our need to understand ourselves as sexual beings doesn't end here. Throughout our lives we may use our dreams to help work out particular aspects of sexuality of which we are unsure, or to release sexual urges that may be

buried under taboo, or that we have not had the opportunity to express. We may dream of fetishes, or have homosexual fantasies, and in so doing uncover sexual impulses that are real for us, or play with ideas that we are curious about but don't want to act out in real life. Acting out the role of the opposite sex may give us an understanding of how our own sexuality may be experienced by our partner. Many people are self-conscious about their bodies, and it can be liberating to have dreams in which they can enjoy sex. Our erotic dreams can enable us to discover and fulfil our sexuality in a positive way.

ABOVE Our sexual fantasies will often be played out in our dreams. Having sex on a train is a fairly common fantasy. **ABOVE LEFT** Talking about sexual problems is a sensitive area, so we may dream about them to help us work them out. **ABOVE FAR LEFT** Our dreams can provide a "safe space" where we can allow and explore sexual feelings.

BELOW It may be easier to enjoy "perfect" sex in our dreams than in our actual relationships. This could be because our inhibitions don't get in the way and our partner seems to know exactly how to give us pleasure. Sharing intimate dreams with your partner can help build trust.

IMPOTENCE DREAM

"I was in a fencing tournament, and my opponent was my boss. I had already donned my mask and jacket, but while my boss was ready and waiting with his sabre raised, I couldn't find mine anywhere.

I had been unable to have an erection for some time, but this dream made me realize that it was the stress of work that was making me impotent."

HEALTHY BODY

Our relationship with our body is often fraught, as our society seems to become more and more obsessed with the way we look rather than how healthy we are. We have manic sessions at the gym, or go on faddy diets and worry about being overweight or dislike parts of our body. These anxieties may come through into our dreams. On the other hand, a general sense of health and vitality in a dream may indicate emotional wellbeing, or at least the desire for it. In dreams where our attention is drawn to a particular part of the body, it could be a reference to what it enables us to do rather than the organ or limb itself.

HEALTH AND WELLBEING

Occasionally we might get dreams in which we are healthy, vibrant, and full of life. Our unconscious does throw up unexpectedly good dreams from time to time to make us realize what we do in fact possess, and although they lack drama and are easily overlooked, these dreams are just as important as dreams of pain or illness.

If we suffer from ill health, such dreams can seem cruel, but they are our unconscious mind's way of instilling hope in us, of showing us that we can overcome anything, even if only in spirit. Dreams such as this can be seen as a call to get better, to find out what is behind our condition and do something about it if possible. If, in our waking life, we are in good health then these dreams may unfold to give us clues to what our unconscious believes is our true potential.

DIET AND EXERCISE

Achieving and maintaining a beautiful, healthy body is a major preoccupation in Western society, and as such it may figure strongly in our nightly dreams if we are dissatisfied with ourselves in some way. The dissatisfaction could be an expression of low self-esteem or of control issues, as both diet and exercise involve discipline and perseverance.

While obesity may signal hanging on to comforts, dieting could suggest that you are depriving yourself in some way, and breaking a diet may be either a loss of control or a defiance of restrictions in your life. If you are exercising in your dream, this could be an indication that you are taking your own needs seriously and feeling the power of your physical being.

THE BODY

Focusing on a particular aspect of your body generally shows a preoccupation with the functionality of that body part or associations commonly made with it. So the head may symbolize your ability to think and rationalize, while the face can be seen as the front you display to the world, as well as being the most intricately expressive part of your body. The heart was long thought to be the seat of our emotions and still holds that association; it can also be thought of as our essential self, associated as it is with the

BELOW FAR RIGHT Therapeutic dreams where you are pampered and cared for might point to an absence of this in your life.
BELOW RIGHT Dreaming of a fast-moving sport might indicate that you want more action and movement in your life.
BELOW A dream in which you are enjoying the invigorating effect of exercise might simply be a dream to enjoy and nothing more.

DREAM OF HEALTH

"I hadn't really noticed that my arthritis was getting worse until I had my 'jumping dream'. In this dream, I was taking vast, bounding leaps like a man on the moon. I felt so fit, so alive, so full of energy. It was an amazing dream and very inspiring. When I woke up I realized just how much pain I was in. My 'jumping dream' made me determined to get rid of it completely, and I became much more assertive and actively involved in making myself well again. I don't think I would have done anything if I hadn't had that dream."

bloodstream, the life force of the body. Hands and feet, arms and legs may be equated with action, movement and dexterity, with being able to go places and do things. Focusing your attention on the eyes, ears, nose or tongue is probably to do with the senses of sight, hearing, smell and taste, and the process of taking in information. Dreaming of the mouth or tongue might also suggest the power of speech.

We may pick up on common metaphors to do with the body when dreaming – "swallowing" information indicates gullibility, while being able to "stomach" something shows a level of tolerance for something we may not like – that we find "distasteful" or "unsavoury".

In our dreams our organs or limbs may not be in their normal state – perhaps they are injured, enlarged or shrunken, or unable to do their job properly. We may dream of having something stuck in our throat, of losing blood or seeing a pool of it. Perhaps images such as these are trying to draw our attention to some level of dysfunctionality, obstacle or imbalance in our lives.

PARALYSIS

Much like a woman who came to Freud's practice complaining of inexplicable paralysis, we are expressing our feelings of powerlessness and vulnerability in our dreams when we lose our ability to move. It may be that we are stuck in some undesirable situation and need some kind of impetus to get ourselves out of it, or that despite all the efforts we have made, we feel frustrated at getting nowhere. Dreams like this may not offer up a complete solution but might help you focus on the problem.

ABOVE Dreaming of being at one with your body and mind is a good wake-up call. Perhaps our dreams can disengage us from our obsession with weight, youth and beauty and help us value what we have.

BELOW FAR LEFT Dreams of ill health often flag an underlying worry we have in our waking lives.
BELOW LEFT Dreaming of the pleasant glow after exercise may start you on the road to a fitter life.
BELOW If you dream of healthy food perhaps you need nourishment. You might also dream of food if you are obsessed with diet and weight control.

Pain and Illness

WHEN WE ARE ASLEEP ANY PAIN OR DISEASE WE HAVE IN OUR BODY OR MIND WILL FILTER THROUGH INTO OUR DREAMS AND BE EXPRESSED EITHER DIRECTLY OR METAPHORICALLY. CONVERSELY, EMOTIONAL DISTRESS WE MAY BE EXPERIENCING IN OUR LIVES MAY MANIFEST IN A DREAM AS PHYSICAL PAIN OR INJURY. DOCTORS AND OTHER MEDICAL STAFF THAT APPEAR IN OUR DREAMS MAY BE THERE TO HELP OR HINDER OUR PROGRESS TO HEALTH, WHILE DREAMING OF BEING IN HOSPITAL COULD BE SEEN AS AN ACKNOWLEDGEMENT OF THE SERIOUSNESS OF A CONDITION. DREAMING OF PAIN AND ILLNESS MAY ALSO BE A METAPHOR FOR SOMETHING ELSE IN YOUR LIFE, AN EMOTIONAL AILMENT FOR EXAMPLE.

74

MIND, BODY AND SPIRIT

RIGHT If we are suffering from pain in real life, then it wouldn't be a surprise if our dream reflected this. If we go to bed with a headache the pain might filter through into our sleep, so we dream of it.

DREAM OF ILL HEALTH

"In my dream I was ill and the doctor was applying leeches. These black slimy things were literally sucking the lifeblood out of me. I woke up feeling quite nauseous. The dream prompted me to look at my new relationship: although my new partner seemed a loving and caring person, as a doctor ought to be, I felt she was using me financially. The blood in the dream was money, and I was letting my partner bleed me dry."

PAIN

In India there is a widespread belief that dreaming about pain in any part of your body indicates that something is wrong with that part; even if a doctor finds nothing wrong it is taken as a sign that this is where pain will get to you sooner or later. But dreams are seldom prophetic, so dreaming of pain doesn't necessarily mean that an injury is going to befall you, although it is possible that your body is trying to tell you that you are ill. If you dream of pain, note what sort of pain you experience and where it is located, and consider what it could be telling you. Also look at what you do about the pain in your dream.

If dreams of pain crop up often, pay special attention to them as they are almost certainly highlighting an area of some importance to your unconscious and may well be your mind's way of expressing emotional rather than physical pain. How we respond to painful or frightening experiences can have major repercussions – they may lead to growth and wisdom, but they can also cause us to retreat to a space that seems safe but is actually stultifying, and prevent us from growing into new awareness.

INJURIES AND ILLNESS

Your body is often symbolic of the self, so any illness or injury that affects your body in your dream is one that affects you as a person. Bruises and cuts may be symbolic of emotional bumps and scrapes, cancers of emotional malignancy, festering wounds of problems that are getting worse, blindness of not seeing or not wanting to look at something.

The fear of being seriously ill is common and we may act it out while we sleep. But the health problems in our dreams are often not life-threatening. Colds, diarrhoea, spots, rashes and warts, for instance, may be uncomfortable, embarrassing or irritating rather than painful, and suggest such discomforts in your life. You may resent being ill, perhaps being too busy to make the time or effort to look after your body. What you feel in your dream about your illness may well be what you are feeling in waking life, and your dream is a way of getting this feeling out into the open.

THE MEDICAL WORLD

If you are given medication in your dream, it is important to note how you respond to receiving it. It may seem like a gift of health, or a poison in disguise; if you don't know what it is then it may bring up control or trust issues for you. Take note of the form the medicine comes in, as well as who gives it to you, and what your relationship is to that person. Receiving an anaesthetic could suggest an emotional numbness or a kind of unconsciousness in your waking life, while surgery may indicate that drastic action is needed around some problem, or that

ABOVE How we view pain and illness – and how we would cope with being confined to bed – can be reflected in our dreams.

BELOW If we have real underlying fear of needles or even doctors, then our dreams may well reflect this.

ABOVE If we are taking medication that we don't really understand, or which may have side effects that we feel ill-prepared for, it will worry us in our dreams.

someone is already taking it for you. Many people may be involved in our dream illness – doctors and nurses, hospital porters and ambulance staff, to name a few. What role do these people have in your dream? Do they take charge, or are they bystanders? If medical personnel are not actually helping you, you may feel let down, and it could be useful to see if this is reflecting something you are experiencing in your life. Depending on your relationship to such figures in your own life, they may well represent the wish to be looked after, to hand over responsibility for your wellbeing to someone who you think is better qualified than you.

A dream that takes place in a hospital may suggest more significant problems in your life or more serious concerns with illness. As an environment a hospital may be alien and frightening, and one in which you have to relinquish much of your control. Many people fear that they will never leave a hospital alive, so it may also indicate that you are facing up to your mortality.

RIGHT Dreaming of a cold might not be a simple reflection of our physical state in real life. It might be a metaphor for something.

BELOW Medical tools can seem intimidating and invasive. If we dream of these perhaps they are symbolic of something in our lives that we feel threatened by.

MADNESS AND IRRATIONALITY

DREAMS ARE SOMETIMES THOUGHT TO BE THE WORKINGS OF A MIND GONE TEMPORARILY INSANE, BUT ACTUALLY BEING IN THE GRIP OF INSANITY RARELY SHOWS ANY SIMILARITY TO OUR DREAMS. THE DREAMING MIND USES METAPHORS AND ALLEGORIES, IMAGES THAT MAY BE QUITE FANTASTICAL AND DISTORTED, AND OPERATES FROM A DIFFERENT LOGICAL BASIS, WHILE IN MADNESS IT IS RATHER A PERSON'S PERCEPTIONS OF WHAT THEY SEE OR HEAR OR FEEL THAT MAY BE DISTORTED. MADNESS IS NOT ONLY USED AS A MEDICAL TERM. WE MAY ALSO BE REFERRING TO OBSESSION OR PARANOIA IN OUR DREAMS; EVEN EXTREMES OF ANGER AND EMOTIONAL INSTABILITY MAY IN SOME CASES BE TERMED INSANITY.

LOGIC AND RATIONALITY

Some of our dreams may seem just like scenes from our waking lives, but at times a different logic from that of our daily lives operates, and rationality and reason seem to be suspended. But if we look more closely, within what seems to be random and meaningless nonsense there may exist a less obvious form of rationality, and within apparently demented or uncontrolled behaviour there is a degree of meaning and purpose.

Our dreams talk to us using symbols and metaphors, and we must try to understand them with our heart, not our head, to feel intuitively what these dreams might mean rather than trying to reason them out. However odd they may be, they are seldom a sign of actual madness. Rather they show the unconscious mind hard at work, producing attention-grabbing images and situations that give us a new way of looking at ourselves, however strange they may seem to our rational mind.

MADNESS

It is hard for sane people to comprehend what it is to be mad, and so in their dreams they may resort to stereotypical imagery to convey the impression of it. Even still, the terms "mad" and "sane" are difficult to define absolutely, as what is right and normal for one individual may be completely wrong or highly bizarre for another.

Madness can take many forms, and in our dreams, being insane may be showing us in an extreme way the levels of distress or confusion we are enduring in our lives and warning us to take action. If you are rather confused, dazed and incoherent in your dreams, you may need to look at how confusion may be distressing you in your waking life, or why you are unable to express yourself clearly.

ASYLUM

Finding ourselves in some kind of mental institution, or asylum, in our dreams may mean that we have acknowledged that we need help, and that we have given ourselves permission to devote our full attention to working through why we feel mad or unstable. Here we will also find ourselves thrown together with others who are insane, and this becomes the normality within the context of the asylum, and gives us a chance to benchmark our feelings and behaviours against others. By dreaming of being institutionalized, we may be showing a need to be helped or looked after, or we could be fighting against the label of madness or the norms of society.

BELOW It is hard for some people to understand the fears that other people have about mental illness, fears that may surface in their dreams in the most negative ways. Try to examine these fears if you suffer from such dreams.

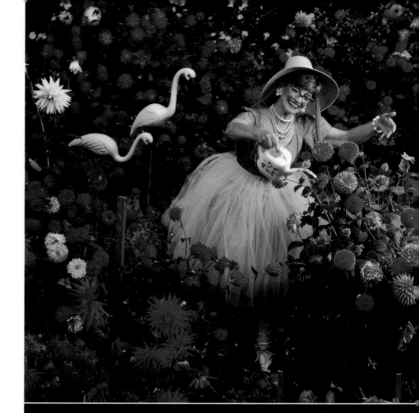

ECCENTRICITY

Odd behaviour in a dream may be disturbing, especially if it is manifesting in someone you know well. Examine how the behaviour is different from that person's normal way of being, as it could be showing you some aspect of your own character that is asking for greater expression. For instance, dreaming of aggression in a person who is normally calm and controlled, or childish behaviour in someone you regard as mature and responsible, may be a way of letting yourself "try out" these behaviours, to see how they feel and how you respond, before you deal with them in reality.

OBSESSION AND PARANOIA

Being fixated on something or someone in our dreams is relatively common, and may reflect a naturally obsessional personal style, or it could be a signal to your conscious mind that there is something you either need to focus your attention on or have been paying too much attention to – only the contexts of your dream and your life will tell you which. The irrational fears that all too often visit our dreams may seem like paranoia, but are likely to be an accentuated form of some real fears, or an indication that we are overly concerned with other people's views of ourselves.

BEING POSSESSED

Madness can take more frightening forms though. Being possessed by devils, or wreaking

RIGHT Extreme flights of fancy and levels of absurdity can seem quite unremarkable in our dreams but totally ridiculous when we wake up and remember the details.
MIDDLE RIGHT However strange a dream may be it is rarely a sign of actual insanity. Instead they present an alternative way of looking at reality.
BOTTOM RIGHT A dream that focuses on some kind of distortion of reality that you find disturbing might be pinpointing your fear of being out of control or letting yourself go.

havoc in a frenzy of unbridled anger, may well affect people who have difficulty coming to terms with their own anger, or who have not found appropriate and satisfying ways of expressing their anger.

SPLIT PERSONALITY AND THE PSYCHOPATH

Sometimes a person's negative feelings can be so strong that they can only cope by cutting off from them. In a way this is what we often do in our dreams by using another character to represent an aspect of ourselves, but if we actually dream of having a split personality then it could be that reconciling two aspects of ourselves that are at odds with each other is our prime task, and it is important to find out what these are. In extreme instances, being cut off from our humanity can manifest as psychopathic behaviour: unstable and violent, the psychopath is unable to form normal personal relationships and may act in anti-social ways, indifferent to his effects on people or his obligations to society as a whole.

SPIRITUALITY AND RELIGION

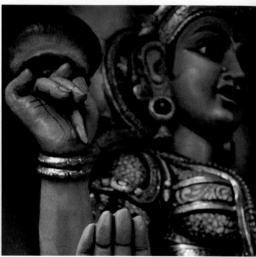

ABOVE We may follow a mainstream religion in our real life, but our dreams may tell us a great deal more about our spirituality if we will look and listen to them.
ABOVE RIGHT The culture and faith we have been brought up in will dictate a lot of what our dreams will be about.

RELIGION GIVES US A FORMALIZED EXPRESSION OF OUR SPIRITUALITY AND PROVIDES A FRAMEWORK FOR OUR BELIEFS. IT IS ALSO ABOUT PRACTICE, AND IN OUR DREAMS WE MAY USE THE RITUALS AND MATERIAL TRAPPINGS OF RELIGION — PRAYER, CHURCHES AND TEMPLES, RELIGIOUS ICONS — AS POINTERS TO SPIRITUAL AND ETHICAL ISSUES. DREAMS OF RELIGION AND SPIRITUAL EXPERIENCES CAN ACT AS PROMPTS FOR US TO INVESTIGATE SOME FUNDAMENTAL QUESTIONS ABOUT OUR EXISTENCE — TO GO BEYOND THE MUNDANE BUSINESS OF OUR DAY-TO-DAY ACTIVITIES.

In a religious dream we may have an experience of true faith, of belief. We may pray to and worship our God; meet divinities face to face; meditate alone or communicate with a priest or religious leader, we may be out in the wilderness or exist in the heart of a congregation.

The Hindus call religious dreams *satsang* dreams – "words of truth" – and believe that some aspect of true divinity does actually speak words of truth to us in our dreams. But our dreams of religion are also telling us about ourselves – our beliefs, our hopes and fears, and our values. They give us the freedom to leave behind all the trappings of our material life and fling ourselves headlong into a truly spiritual way of being, and in so doing, to learn and grow.

BELIEF SYSTEMS

Our own faith, if any, will have a strong bearing on what we dream about and how we perceive the content of our dream, but while we are more likely to create a familiar faith or belief setting in our dream it doesn't necessarily mean that we will never explore and examine other belief systems in our dreams. If we do, such dreams may offer new perspectives to our own, enriching and strengthening our beliefs or challenging them and giving us new insights.

THE AFTERLIFE

The older we get the more likely we are to have religious dreams, even if we studiously avoid spiritual issues in waking life, as they are often a reminder from the unconscious mind of our mortality. We may increasingly feel the need to explore what happens after we die, and turn to belief in the afterlife as a happier option than oblivion.

MORALITY – A BALANCING ACT

Goodness and evil, sins and forgiveness, charity and mercy – these are issues that form the focus of many a religious upbringing. While some people derive peace and comfort from religion, the abundance of these very concepts may engender rather a generalized feeling of guilt and a fear of not being good enough. Religious dreams may give us the wherewithal to feel that we are forgiven, cleansed of our faults and sins, and also to find out whether we are on the right moral track.

PRAYER

In our dreams, praying may mean many things. Prayers and sacrifices can be seen as a means of atonement or a way of bargaining with the gods; if this seems true for you, see if there is something you really want, and what you are sacrificing in order to get it. Through prayer and meditation we may be trying not only to communicate with God, but also to connect with a higher aspect of ourselves, with our own spiritual core.

THE HOUSE OF GOD

Places of worship throughout the world are usually easily recognizable, and they could figure in your dreams both as the physical representation of a particular faith, or as a place where you feel you can get in touch with your spiritual self or be closer to God. Note whether the building in your dreams provides you with an intimate environment, or if it is vast and awe-inspiring, making you feel small and insignificant in the face of a great deity.

RELIGIOUS LEADERS

Spiritual leaders can be complex figures to whom we respond in many ways. We often see them as authority figures, whether they are the kind, wise and insightful type who can guide us through spiritual and emotional turmoil, or distant ceremonial figures representing power and even material wealth. We may engage with these leaders on an individual basis, reminiscent of parent-child interaction, or receive their communication as part of a large congregation.

THE RELIGIOUS COMMUNITY

Religion can provide us with an instant community, a group of people with whom we share, to a greater or lesser extent, our spiritual beliefs and values. Socially these people can be immensely important to us, and we may define ourselves by belonging with them and by the rituals we engage in together.

Because religion and morality often go hand in hand, a congregation or other religious grouping in your dream may indicate social judgement, so it will be important to look at how you fit in with this community – if you are accepted or an outcast.

If the community is an evangelical one and you feel comfortable participating in spreading the word, it could be a sign that you have a message to get across, something that you want to tell the world at large.

ABOVE Religion can cement us to our community. Spirituality can set us free.
ABOVE LEFT Whatever religious figures we have been brought up with will often appear in our dreams as messengers.
ABOVE FAR LEFT Dreams of church buildings or icons might indicate a sense that we feel we need to atone or repent in some way.

RIGHT All faiths come complete with their own particular icons.

ENGAGING WITH PEOPLE

Of all the elements we are likely to encounter in our dreams it is people that will feature most often. At times in our waking life we respond to people strongly, falling passionately in love or running into conflict, and without them we can become lonely. Usually when a person appears in a dream their significance is unique and relevant in the context of that dream alone, although if you have a series of dreams on the same theme they might become representative of something particular – some aspect of yourself, or an archetypal figure. Besides the characters that you meet in your dreams there is always you, the observer or participant.

Many of the activities that fill our lives revolve around people. We keep busy for many reasons – sociability, fun or fitness, out of curiosity or necessity – and in our dreams we can continue to explore, to do things we can't do in real life, or to work through issues that are troubling us in our day-to-day lives.

FAMILY

THE MEMBERS OF OUR FAMILY ARE POTENTIALLY THE CLOSEST PEOPLE TO US. THEY ARE WITH US FROM BIRTH, WE GROW UP WITH THEM, WE KNOW THEM INTIMATELY AND, HOPEFULLY, LOVE THEM DEARLY. WE SPEND A LOT OF TIME WITH OUR FAMILY, AND THIS CAN CREATE BOTH A WONDERFUL CLOSENESS AND TREMENDOUS STRESS. THERE CAN BE MORE CONFLICT BETWEEN FAMILY MEMBERS THAN ANY OTHER RELATIONSHIP. AT SOME TIMES IN OUR LIFE THE BONDS CAN BE STRETCHED TO BREAKING POINT, AND AT OTHERS THERE IS A DISTANCE THAT YOU FEEL RECONCILED TO BUT WHICH IN FACT IS SUBCONSCIOUSLY BOTHERING YOU. IT IS HARDLY SURPRISING THAT THE FAMILY FEATURES FREQUENTLY IN OUR DREAMS.

ABOVE The concept of family, and the individuals within it, is a powerful force and will figure large in our dreams. Our parents will be the most influential aspect for most of us.

Family members are irreplaceable – while friends and acquaintances may come and go, if we lose a parent or grandparent, child or sibling, or if we fall out with them irrevocably, their role can never be taken by someone else. Thus when we do get into conflict situations with them there is a lot at stake. If we are unwilling or unable to resolve issues effectively, they almost inevitably surface in our dreams.

The family can be seen as a microcosm of society, and in it we learn to understand social roles and behaviours, and establish core norms and values.

Our responses to authority, power, love, companionship and many other aspects of human behaviour and social structures will be learnt in the family and taken with us into society. Because of this, dreaming of a family member might often be pointing towards a characteristic rather than a dream about that person. For example, if you felt that your father was a forbidding and authoritarian element in your childhood, in your dream his presence might actually be a reference to a real-life bullying boss you are having difficulty with at work.

PARENTS

Our parents are probably the most influential people in our lives. We are heavily dependent on them during our early years, and they are an important source of information about the world. We also learn from them a vast array of attitudes and behaviours that may help us to integrate into society or that may be dysfunctional and present us with constant difficulties.

Our relationship with our parents evolves through childhood and changes during our adult years as we mature, and as they grow old and perhaps dependent. In dreams of our parents we are often trying to

work through unresolved childhood issues and how they continue to affect us as adults. For instance, a child that is often punished for something they haven't done may carry unjustified feelings of guilt with them for the rest of their lives. On the other hand the appearance of your parents in your dream may suggest that you are feeling a need to be loved and looked after if your parents are loving and nurturing people.

CHILDREN

Many parents expend a lot of energy on worrying about their children. They may take these worries to be bed with them, exaggerating them in their dreams, as they play out worst-case scenarios as a way of anticipating and preparing for unexpected or difficult situations. It is also quite possible that you are unconsciously aware of some difficulty with your child, and your unconscious is trying to bring this to your attention.

Dreaming about our own children after they have grown up might be an attempt to go back and change something we did, to put it to rights, and in so doing to absolve our feelings of guilt about the mistakes we made as a parent. If we can see what aspect of our parenting is

ABOVE Position and hierarchy within the family group might still affect us even when we've moved away from home.

disquieting us, we can to try to make amends. We can also relive the joy of our own childhood through our children, updating and perhaps improving on the experiences that we had ourselves. Our children can show us how our childhood might have been, and how we can get in touch with the child within us, giving us the opportunity to recapture the freedom and innocence of our early years. Much will depend on the nature of your own childhood and on how you relate to your children.

LEFT If our childhood was happy then we will find any dreams of it will also be happy – and we can just enjoy them.

BELOW If on the other hand our childhood was less than safe, or we still have unresolved fears about it, our dreams may also make us feel unsafe.

BROTHERS AND SISTERS

Sibling relationships are particularly complex because we may feel some ambivalence around our brothers and sisters. On the one hand they are our constant companions during childhood – we share our experiences, we play games and have jokes with each other, we have the same family situation, and so are often in a position to understand and empathize with each other more than anyone else. For a younger child, older siblings can be invaluable role models and teachers as well.

However, sibling rivalry should never be underestimated – the first-born may always at some level resent the loss of parental attention that the birth of younger siblings inevitably brings, and constant comparisons by parents and teachers can be irksome, depriving a child of their individuality and potentially bringing a sense of inadequacy.

Dreams of siblings can underscore these feelings and allow us to address buried resentments, perhaps by being more assertive. Your brother or sister may have qualities that you wish to bring out in yourself, and their presence in your dream may be an attempt to do this.

FRIENDS

THE FRIENDSHIPS WE HAVE OCCUR AT MANY LEVELS, FROM SUPERFICIAL ACQUAINTANCES TO LIFELONG COMPANIONS. CIRCUMSTANTIAL FRIENDSHIPS — SUCH AS THE COLLEAGUES WE LIKE AND WITH WHOM WE MAY OCCASIONALLY HAVE A CHAT, OR THE PEOPLE WE MEET AT NIGHT SCHOOL — MAY DEVELOP, BUT BASICALLY THEY ARE ON THE OUTSIDE OF OUR NETWORK. AT THE OTHER END OF THE SPECTRUM ARE THE PEOPLE WHO ARE OUR CLOSEST COMPANIONS, PEOPLE WE REALLY CONNECT WITH ON A DEEP LEVEL, OR WITH WHOM WE HAVE SO MUCH SHARED HISTORY THAT OUR DIFFERENCES BECOME IRRELEVANT. DREAMS OF FRIENDS MAY BE OF EITHER SORT, AND WILL HAVE SIMILARLY DIFFERENT LEVELS.

We relate to our friends on different levels, sharing deeply personal things with them and relying on them in difficult times or simply having a good time and a laugh with each other. We may have a lot in common with them, or be completely at odds with them in many ways but still value their companionship. Because our relationships with our friends are so diverse, they can mean many things to us when they appear in our dreams.

FRIENDS IN OUR DREAMS

We choose our friends, responding to aspects of their personality or shared experiences that we can relate to, and because of this they may sometimes be closer to us than our relatives. Friends become all the more important if your family is not loving and supportive, and can in some cases provide a kind of substitute family. But we also befriend people with whom we share common activities or interests, and this may be the focus of the relationship rather than any deeply shared personal connection with them.

We may dream of friends for many reasons – out of love or guilt, or in order to resolve conflict issues. If the friend you dream of is associated with an activity such as a sport or hobby, then it could be some aspect of the activity rather than the qualities of that person that you are investigating. With closer friends though, we often dream of them because they have a particular quality on which we need to focus our attention, perhaps to understand it, adopt it ourselves, or reject it.

> ### DREAM OF A FRIEND
> "I hadn't seen my friend Paul for a long time. He'd been abroad teaching and I guess I missed him. I dreamt that he was back and we were on his motorbike together. He turned to me to say something and didn't see there was a lorry coming towards us. We crashed and I woke up. I was concerned at the time because I hadn't heard from him in such a long time and I think I was worrying that something might have happened to him. I didn't know if anyone would think to let me know. On another level it could have been that I was worrying about our friendship having 'died'."

BELOW RIGHT We all need friends and companions to be a healthy part of society. We might take it for granted in our waking lives, but celebrate it in our dreams, however bizarrely.
BELOW A friendship dream doesn't have to be particularly profound, but might simply highlight the importance of a friend's presence in your life.

FRIENDS OR STRANGERS?

Sometimes in our dreams our friends will be transformed into unfamiliar people – so much so that we are not sure whether or not they are still the same person that we know and love. Such transformations draw our attention to the differences – so for example, if a friend who is always bouncy and jovial appears in your dream in tears, this may be a sign that you have lost touch with the positive things in life, that you need to reconnect with what makes you happy and perhaps with the people that you really enjoy being with.

LOSING A FRIEND

Such transformations may also be our unconscious mind's way of working out how we feel about relationships. Friendships are often fragile and changeable, and can easily evaporate if we don't take care of them or if our circumstances change or we develop in different ways.

Having friends can make us feel valued, and the loss of a friendship can be a heavy blow. If we do lose contact it might be no more than an accident but it still hurts, and we still feel the loss. Dreams may be a way of coming to terms with such losses, or of bringing determination to putting a friendship back on track.

LEFT A good social life is an essential part of a happy and wholesome life; it emphasizes the positive. Just as close one-to-one friendships are vital, so are groups of friends where a different dynamic exists.

BELOW LEFT We may feel the loss of friends long after they have grown away, and remember them in our dreams.
BELOW In childhood we begin to establish friendships that may last us a lifetime.

Let us learn to dream, gentlemen, and then we may perhaps find the truth.

F. A. KEKULÉ

LOVERS

FINDING AND RELATING TO A LOVER IS ONE OF THE BIG PREOCCUPATIONS OF ADULTHOOD. IF WE DON'T HAVE A LOVER WE
PROBABLY WANT ONE, AND IF WE DO, WE MAY DREAM OF THEM TO REINFORCE HOW WONDERFUL IT IS TO BE IN LOVE, OR
TO WORK THROUGH THE CONFLICT ISSUES THAT INEVITABLY CROP UP FROM TIME TO TIME. WE MAY DREAM NOT ONLY OF
OUR CURRENT PARTNER, BUT ALSO OF PAST LOVES, OR OF PEOPLE WE ARE ATTRACTED TO BUT WHO ARE UNAVAILABLE; WE
MAY EVEN HAVE FANTASIES ABOUT COMPLETELY UNATTAINABLE LOVE OBJECTS. IF WE STIFLE OUR LOVE FANTASIES OR AVOID
LOOKING AT DIFFICULT RELATIONSHIP ISSUES CONSCIOUSLY, THIS MAY WELL SURFACE IN OUR DREAMS.

PAST LOVERS

It is quite common to dream of past lovers. It may mean that you are hankering after being with them again, but often it is simply your unconscious mind's way of cataloguing and storing away experiences and memories. Often it is important that you process why a relationship ended so that you don't make the same mistakes again with the next person. You may need to regain a level of self-esteem after a damaging or abusive relationship, and realize that it is alright to be just who you are.

Whatever it is you need to work through, dreams give you the opportunity to do so.

BELOW Our notions of what makes a romantic situation are often conditioned by our culture, and the standard ideals may surface in our dreams as our mind replays the images we have absorbed.

PRESENT LOVERS

Just as we dream about our friends and family on a fairly regular basis, so too do we dream of our present partner. There are many reasons for this. It can be our unconscious mind's way of reassuring ourselves that we are still loved. Even playing with notions of being unfaithful or out of love, or being cruel, hurtful, or distant may be our unconscious mind's way of checking that things are in reality alright, or of experimenting with ideas or situations without us having to try anything out for real.

Unpleasant dreams about a lover may also hint at a certain dissatisfaction in a relationship, and give you an opportunity to see how it might be to behave differently from the way you do in real life.

POTENTIAL LOVERS

Our unconscious likes to keep an open mind on what is around us. This may be unsettling if you are in a good relationship, but it is also normal and natural. Just because we dream about people we fancy doesn't mean we would do anything about it in our waking life or even that we want to. It may be just a way of experimenting with the idea without having to go there. It may also mean that unhappiness in your relationship is prompting you to see a way to finding a more satisfactory partner.

FANTASY LOVERS

The most common fantasy lovers in our dreams are real people whom we might, in an ideal world, make a play for, but with whom a relationship is at best extremely unlikely. These might be people in the public eye, like pop stars or actors, or people with whom it would be too risky to have an actual relationship, such as a boss or married person.

When we are asleep there is no limit to our imagination, and occasionally the lovers of our dreams may be really bizarre and

RIGHT Dreaming of having an affair might reflect a desire you have for the unknown.
MIDDLE RIGHT Dreaming of your love life could be a way of working through the everyday concerns of any relationship.
BOTTOM RIGHT Dreams of a romantic new affair can simply be highly enjoyable escapism.

completely unobtainable. We may also dream of breaking taboos, and have sexual dreams involving incest, or animals, for instance. Many people might be shocked by having such fantasies, and for some they may be an indication of disturbed psychological states, in which case professional help may be needed. For the most part though, our unconscious likes to slip the leash occasionally and dream of things we would simply never do – it does not mean that we would want to act these out in reality. Our dreams are a way of approaching taboos in safety, experimenting or letting off sexual steam. The meaning will depend on who we are – it could be that we are reacting to social restrictions and trying to find greater freedom of expression; in fact breaking taboos in dreams may be a liberating experience.

If you are the kind of person who worries what others think of you this may be disturbing. In our dream we may need to deal with others being judgemental, or even with our own self-condemnation, if we take unusual or inappropriate lovers. But a taboo lover may also be a companion on your journey to self-fulfilment and have qualities that you don't find elsewhere.

DREAM OF LOVERS

"I had about half a dozen dreams about my boss, who I rather fancied. They were never exactly the same, but they always involved being physically intimate, and always one or other of us was a reluctant partner in this intimacy, usually because we were afraid of discovery.

I think that this dream was my way of attaining something that in reality would never be possible. I think that the reluctance was to do with my fear that my own partner would find out that I was attracted to someone else, as well as with the fact that my boss was in reality very happily married. "

PEOPLE IN OUR LIVES

IN GOING ABOUT THE DAY-TO-DAY BUSINESS OF OUR LIVES, WE ENGAGE WITH COUNTLESS PEOPLE. OUR ENCOUNTERS WITH THEM MAY BE INSIGNIFICANT OR TRIVIAL – THE FELLOW PASSENGERS YOU SIT BESIDE IN SILENCE DURING A TRAIN JOURNEY AND NEVER SEE AGAIN, THE CHECKOUT OPERATOR IN AN UNEVENTFUL VISIT TO THE SUPERMARKET – OR THEY COULD BE MORE INVOLVED, SUCH AS THE RELATIONSHIPS THAT DEVELOP WITH COLLEAGUES OR NEIGHBOURS. WE EVEN HAVE A RELATIONSHIP OF SORTS WITH FAMOUS PEOPLE WHOSE FACES ARE FAMILIAR AND WHOSE LIVES WE MIGHT READ ABOUT, BUT WHO WE MAY NEVER MEET.

RIGHT Whoever we are intimidated by in our everyday waking life is likely to "visit" us in our dreams in a similar way. If this happens repeatedly you might want to work with why this person affects you so deeply.

Any of these people could appear as characters in our dreams, whether they are playing supporting roles or taking the lead, and although at times they may simply be a necessary part of the scenery, like extras in a film, they will often appear in our dreams for a reason. Notice what role they play, as well as how you behave towards each other in the dream and how you feel during and after the interaction.

FAMILIAR FACES

In going about the routine of our lives, we get to know many faces in the places we frequent – neighbours, the people who work in the local shops or bank, the people we work and socialise with and countless others. When such people appear in a dream,

try to establish whether it is their role that seems important or their personal qualities. For instance, a neighbour may have to do with having your privacy and personal space invaded, or it may be reminding you that there are friendly people about who are always willing to help you. Dreaming of your boss is quite likely to be about issues of power, authority, status and so on, but it may be that the formal relationship you have with each other is secondary to particular personality traits that you feel he or she exhibits.

IN THE PUBLIC GAZE

Royalty and politicians, media celebrities, and others who have made it into the public arena may all feature in our dream

world. As we only know them from a distance, it will be the qualities they present to the outside world – their public face – that we probably focus on. This may be simply the fact that they have achieved fame and fortune or infamy, that they have reached the pinnacle of success on their chosen path, or it may be more specifically about what it is that they have done, or how they have gone about getting what they want. We may want their success to rub off on us, to use them as a role model, or to engage with them and turn the one-way relationship into a more personal one.

STRANGERS

What does it mean, though, if the people we encounter in our dreams are not familiar faces, but apparently arbitrary individuals? Realistically, strangers are likely to appear in our dreams as often as they do in real life, but if we do engage with them or something about them grabs our attention particularly, it may be worth looking at whether they have a particular significance to us. It may indeed be the very fact that we don't know them that is salient – we may feel uncertain or wary of them, they may behave in unpredictable or mysterious or dangerous ways, or they may be

BELOW If you dream of people who are famous in real life you are probably dreaming of what they represent to you. Alternatively, maybe there is something about fame itself that intrigues and attracts you?

ABOVE We might all fear crowds, especially if they are made up of strangers, but being part of a mass gathering can also be quite exhilarating.

people we are attracted to and want to get to know. Look at the kind of interaction you have in the dream and how you feel about the contact you have with them. Obviously, a stranger chasing you with a loaded gun will bring up quite different feelings from one who shows you the way when you are lost.

In particular, see what qualities are dominant in your dream, as a stranger could present some aspect of yourself that you have yet to bring to awareness. Also look at whether the person seems to conform to any stereotypes – the tall, dark and handsome stranger who may be the lover of your dreams, or the wise old man or woman who can be your guide or angel.

Strangers who are obviously foreigners or people of different races may bring issues of difference or prejudice to the fore, and whether the person is a man, woman or child could be drawing your attention to your own personal masculine, feminine or childlike qualities that may be useful for you to focus on right now.

ABOVE You have to look at what qualities each person brings to your dream to understand them and their impact on your life.

RIGHT Fear of getting to know people may figure in our dreams and we may seek ways to get round this in our waking life.

BELOW Work colleagues might not be our best friends but we spend a disproportionate amount of time with them, and this dominance in our lives might be reflected in our dreams.

GATHERINGS

ABOVE If you dream about a party at which you feel out of place and lonely, then analyse why this might be so. What kind of party was it? Who was there? What made you feel peripheral?

ABOVE RIGHT A gathering of lots of people in a dream can act as an indicator of how we think we fit into society.

WE GATHER BECAUSE WE ARE SOCIAL BEINGS. WE ALL BELONG TO COMMUNITIES OF VARIOUS DESCRIPTIONS — FAMILY, NEIGHBOURHOOD, WORKPLACE, NATION — AND SHARE RESOURCES, INFORMATION AND COLLECTIVE EXPERIENCES WITH EACH OTHER. WE GET TOGETHER AS A FAMILY, WE MEET COLLEAGUES TO DISCUSS BUSINESS, AND WE JOIN THOUSANDS OF STRANGERS IN PUBLIC FOR A CONCERT OR TO CELEBRATE A NATIONAL EVENT. THE GATHERINGS OF OUR DREAMS REFLECT THIS DIVERSITY, AND THEY ALSO EXPRESS HOW WE FEEL IN THE CONTEXT OF SOCIAL GROUPINGS.

HARMONY

Gatherings where people understand and support each other, and want to be together, can give a tremendous sense of belonging, and help you to feel safe, supported and sustained. If you have been struggling with such issues, dreaming of such a gathering may show that some

aspect of your personal sense of community is now being satisfied in some way.

Harmonious gatherings can also be an expression of general consensus on society's norms and values. Looking in on them from the outside, though, or being excluded from them, could indicate a rejection of these norms, or that you still have some kind of unresolved social issues – isolation, a lack of confidence about your role in your community or workplace, or uncertainty about how accepted you are by the people you value.

Unfortunately, gatherings can also be fraught with discord. Antagonism, dominance or bullying are all too present in our society and you may be using the gathering in your dream as a

metaphor for these. If this is the case, look for any signs of resolution, and also see who is present and what their dominant characteristics are. If you are involved in the dream rather than an onlooker, see what role you are playing.

ROLES

The characters in your dream gathering are probably playing particular roles, perhaps in some kind of hierarchy, or at least contributing to the group identity. They may be people you know or complete strangers – leaders and followers, teachers, diplomats trying to keep the peace and finding solutions to problems, jokers defusing situations with their humour, and the black sheep, pulling in a different direction and at odds

---

A DREAM OF REJECTION

"I was looking through a window into an expensive restaurant. All my friends were gathered together, eating and drinking and having a good time. I became very distressed at not being amongst them. Were they talking about me? Had I not been invited? Had I lost the invitation or been turned away? I banged on the window but no one could hear me. In the dream I became anxious that this was all an elaborate joke; they were pretending to ignore me, and wanted to hurt me.

I had just split up with my partner, who had been quite hurtful. I was feeling insecure and shut out, and my self-esteem had taken a blow."

with everyone. Gatherings may also speak to us of individuality, whether suppressed or given freedom. See what your own role is within the group, how others perceive you, and how you respond to that role as well as to the goals or beliefs of the group.

FORMALITY

Some people like the informality of an unstructured gathering, with its sense of companionship, freedom and youthful energy, while others prefer the more formal circumstances of an organized event. Formality can give us the safety of structure if we understand and feel comfortable with it, but it can also be intimidating if we don't feel we belong.

CROWDS

Being in a large crowd, such as at a major sports match or a New Year celebration, can be an exhilarating experience as the happy, excited mood of the people rubs off on you. But it can also be immensely stressful – even downright scary if the

crowd becomes a mob. Your relationship with the crowd in your dream is important in understanding what it means – does it give you a sense of belonging or community, a unity of purpose, a celebration, or is it threatening, in which case you may panic at the thought of getting crushed, or feel that you need to escape and be alone?

Try to relate this to your everyday life – crowd dreams could be telling you something about the amount and type of contact you are having in relation to your needs as an individual, or

about your relationship with conventions and the mass of opinions. If you tend to need time alone to recharge your batteries and aren't getting this, you may be expressing a need to get away from people for a while. Conversely you may be feeling isolated, and need people around you to make you feel human again. A crowd dream where you can't escape or where the attention of the crowd is focused entirely on you may indicate that you feel pressure to conform rather than taking your own direction in life.

ABOVE Really big crowds can be scary – but that is true in waking life as much as dreams and we shouldn't read too much into such fears.
ABOVE LEFT In a social gathering we may feel "small", which might represent that this is how we feel about ourselves in real life.

BELOW Any crowd scene can represent how we feel about being part of a group. Do you blend in or are you singled out in some way as being other than the norm? Does this please or daunt you? Do you want to conform or rebel?

CELEBRATIONS AND CEREMONIES

CELEBRATIONS CAN TAKE MANY FORMS – FROM SPONTANEOUSLY OPENING A BOTTLE OF CHAMPAGNE WITH A FEW FRIENDS, TO THE FESTIVITIES AND RITUALS OF A RELIGIOUS HOLIDAY OR A FORMAL AND HIGHLY REHEARSED NATIONAL CEREMONY. WHEN WE DREAM OF SUCH CELEBRATIONS THEY ARE LIKELY TO BE EVENTS IN WHICH WE ARE PERSONALLY INVOLVED, ALTHOUGH THE GRAND CEREMONIES OF CELEBRITIES AND LEADERS – A ROYAL WEDDING, THE FUNERAL OF A STATESMAN, OR AN INAUGURATION – MAY FEATURE TOO. OUR DREAMS MIGHT ALSO FEATURE THE SYMBOLS OF THESE CEREMONIES RATHER THAN THE GATHERINGS: A WEDDING RING, AN ELABORATE CAKE, BALLOONS OR STREAMERS MIGHT MAKE AN APPEARANCE.

ABOVE We all like to celebrate and we enjoy having our friends around us to help us party. Our dreams are no different and are to be enjoyed.
ABOVE RIGHT There are a lot of cycles in our life that need to be marked as a rite of passage. You might dream of the symbols that are linked with an event rather than the event itself.

ANTICIPATING AN EVENT

In the build-up to a major life event such as a wedding or the birth of a child, the excitement and apprehension can spill over into our dreams. In dreaming of the event our unconscious attempts to work out the fears we have around it – saying the wrong thing, forgetting something crucial, or making a fool of ourselves in some way. With weddings in particular, we are publicly entering into a social contract and may be anxious about having made the right

decision. Perhaps we are even responsible for the administration of such events, in which case it might be sheer nerves that makes us dream about them. On the positive side, such dreams give you a chance to rehearse and familiarize yourself with the event, and to anticipate things that could go wrong.

CEREMONY AS SYMBOL

Dreams of ceremonies are not necessarily about real events though. If the dream seems to spring out of nowhere we should view the ceremony as a symbol –

probably for the achievement or event that it is designed to mark, or for the feelings that the prospect of such an event evokes. So a 21st birthday party may mean that we are maturing in some way, or feeling the increased freedoms or the responsibilities of adulthood, while a wedding could be prompting us to ask ourselves about our relationship – perhaps about how committed we feel – or if we are single, to explore what kind of person we would like to settle down with.

The exact purpose or structure of the celebration may be less important than the feelings that it brings up in you, and it is worth asking yourself if you fear such events or anticipate them happily. Maybe you want to be the centre of attention but have difficulty reconciling this with being shy or modest, or perhaps you find it stressful making speeches or playing the host or hostess – roles that also put you firmly in the spotlight.

If in your waking life you are being caught up in routine and yearn to be more spontaneous, your dream celebrations could give you the opportunity to let your hair down. If you think this is true then try and create a time where you can do it for real, and live the dream.

THE PARAPHERNALIA OF CELEBRATIONS

More subtle indications or symbols of ceremonies may be present in your dream – a wedding ring standing in for the unity and commitment of marriage, a coffin for the death of a loved one, a crown or sceptre for a coronation, balloons for a festive occasion.

Clothes are an important part of many traditional ceremonies, and if in your dream the clothes are wrong for the occasion, you should look at what makes them so – wearing casual clothes to a formal occasion, for instance, may indicate your resistance to the event, or a feeling that you are not ready for it.

Gift-giving can be fraught with difficulty and evoke a strong emotional response. Look at what the gift is and how appropriate it is, the spirit in which it is given and received, who the recipient and giver are, and, if many presents are changing hands, whether they are comparable or unfairly distributed. Gifts can represent our talents and opportunities, so receiving them or being disappointed by them may hint at how you feel about broader issues in your life.

RIGHT A dream that involves a dramatic or epic celebration on a large scale might indicate that you are fretting about a real-life one you are involved with, or might be highlighting a desire you feel to live a little wildly for a time, and forget about your usual routines.
MIDDLE RIGHT By letting off steam we can release a lot of the tension that such events may induce.
BOTTOM RIGHT A symbol of celebration, such as popping corks, might be a sign or expression of happiness.

RITUAL

Many ceremonies are highly ritualized. Their stylised and formulaic nature means that everyone has a role and knows how to behave. Some rituals are extremely taxing, such as some complex and physically exacting initiation rites, which are a test of stamina, physical prowess and ultimately, of whether the initiate is ready for his or her new role.

In dreams we may try to resolve issues around a role we need to play, and so our unconscious will replay this and try to analyse our response to it. Rituals are often able to give us the comfort of predictability, but they may also be markers of change. Look at whether you are a creature of habit or if you enjoy change, and consider why change features in your dream.

DREAM WEDDING

"I was getting married and all the invitations had been sent out, but in my dream I was trying to post them and they kept turning into scorpions in my hand. The harder I tried to post them the more they fought back and tried to sting me. It was quite terrifying. Although I really wanted to get married, I had had to invite a whole bunch of people that I didn't know – my fiancé's relatives and a lot of my mother's friends and distant relations – and this was where the problem lay. I didn't want them to be there on my big day, and the dream was my way of resisting having to invite them."

SEPARATION

WHETHER IN OUR DREAMS OR IN WAKING LIFE, SEPARATION ALWAYS IMPLIES CHANGES IN OUR LIVES, LETTING GO AND STARTING ANEW. WE MAY TYPICALLY THINK OF PARTING FROM LOVED ONES, BUT THE IDEA CAN EQUALLY BE APPLIED TO LEAVING HOME, ENDING A JOB, GOING ON A JOURNEY, OR A PHASE IN LIFE DRAWING TO A CLOSE. WE MAY HAVE SADNESS AROUND THE SEPARATION AND THE LOSS OF THE LOVED AND THE FAMILIAR, BUT MANY A SEPARATION WILL INSTEAD BRING HAPPINESS, RELIEF OR EXCITEMENT AS WE LOOK AHEAD. DREAMS OF SEPARATION WILL REFLECT ALL THESE ISSUES DIRECTLY, AND CAN ALSO PINPOINT ANXIETIES WE ARE FEELING THAT AREN'T NECESSARILY OBVIOUSLY LINKED TO SEPARATION ANXIETY.

ENGAGING WITH PEOPLE

BELOW LEFT Separation leads to an emotion that goes very deep indeed; we may carry over such deeply held scars all of our life.
BELOW RIGHT Our dreams may reflect such feelings of separation and loneliness, and may need addressing when we are awake in order to find the source, and hopefully alleviate the pain.

PARTING FROM OUR LOVED ONES

It is inevitable that we will at some stage be separated from people we love. As well as coping with the loss, we are afraid of being lonely and having to become self-reliant when perhaps we lack the confidence to do so, and we may give vent to these fears in our dreams. The loss of a long-term relationship is likely to affect us particularly strongly as we grow increasingly dependent on the person whose life is intimately involved with our own, although for some it may come as a relief or a blessing, a way to flourish. Either way we may use dream time to come to terms with the changes and the feelings they bring up.

LEAVING HOME

When leaving our family and home, even temporarily, we have to discover our independence, perhaps for the very first time, we need to stand on our own two feet without the support we are used to. While being a valuable and important voyage of discovery, this may also be hard to deal with.

Students often report disturbed dreams during their first year away from home. These dreams are often about their childhood, as if by dreaming it they can recapture some of the security they felt then, and are possibly missing now. Leaving the past behind in this way provides an opportunity to discover yourself as an adult, without parental constraints, and you may well use your dreams to engage with new issues and lifestyles as much as to separate from and lay to rest your childhood.

DIVORCE

Going through divorce is almost always a traumatic experience, and if you are experiencing this process your dreams will probably reflect your distress. Conflict and haggling over possessions may be scary and worrying, especially if you stand to lose a lot in the divorce. You may feel guilty about having caused your marriage to fall apart, or about not having put in enough effort to make it work — or you may blame your partner for exactly the same things. You

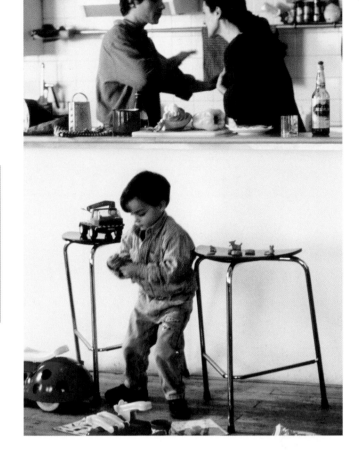

DREAM OF SEPARATION

"I was at a huge fancy-dress ball, dressed in elegant clothing and a golden, feathered mask. As we danced I became aware that everyone was staring and pointing at me and making barbed, accusatory comments. I felt very vulnerable. In real life people had been very understanding and kind about me divorcing and remarrying, but this dream brought home to me what I had done. I started feeling very responsible, very accountable around the divorce."

may even be angry with yourself for having wasted time in the relationship. Coming to terms with our own role in a divorce is part of the long painful process to a new normality, to achieving independence for ourselves.

For many people the worst part is having to be separated from children – both the loss of their presence and guilt at abandoning them. The partner with custody may feel anxiety around having to look after them unaided. How you feel about these issues will affect the quality and content of your dreams.

Divorce is also a traumatic time for children, as they get caught in the cross-fire between the adults involved, and have immensely strong feelings that they are often not able to express or deal with fully. They may feel responsible for the split, abandoned by the parent that leaves, and in some cases fearful and unsettled around the other changes that are happening at the same time, especially if these are not explained fully to them. Children are more prone to nightmares than adults, and may be particularly affected by them at these kinds of stressful times.

MOVING ON

Long-term separation requires a major adjustment, even if there are positive spin-offs. Moving on may mean coming to terms with past issues and letting go of them, and the new start in life could provide the chance to gain or regain our freedom and sense of self. Dreams that involve objects strongly associated with your past, such as favourite childhood toys or gifts given to you by your partner, may well be showing you what you need to let go of.

LEFT Dreaming of going away somewhere, perhaps alone, might point to feelings of separation anxiety that you are trying to subdue. It might also point to a desire to get away and move on.

SEPARATION ANXIETY

At the age of around seven or eight months, a baby starts to show signs of having a strong attachment to its primary carer, and distress when separated from that person, especially when upset or ill.

At first the infant may protest by crying, but can be comforted by another. If the separation is prolonged, the child may despair, seeming calmer but becoming apathetic, no longer looking for its carer and trying to comfort itself by thumb-sucking or rocking. In the most extreme cases of separation anxiety the infant becomes detached and unresponsive, and will even ignore the return of the caregiver.

These very human reactions we have to separation might be at their most acute when we are young, but they can carry on to adulthood, and can perhaps be as traumatic and damaging. Dreams may well bring up these issues, and if you dream of them often, perhaps you need to examine where your anxieties come from.

ABOVE When it is time to move on from an unhappy relationship, the grief of separation can be hard to bear, for all concerned, even if we know it's the best course of action. If a separation you were involved with happened long ago, but is still part of your emotional baggage, you may well deal with it in dreams.

PERFORMANCE

ABOVE In our dreams, the trappings of the ballet could symbolize a desire for fame and a glamorous and "artistic" life.

ABOVE RIGHT To dream that we are taking part in a theatrical performance can reveal how we feel about being on display in the many public roles we play in life.

WHEN WE THINK OF PERFORMANCE WE PROBABLY HAVE SOME KIND OF DRAMATIC PRODUCTION IN MIND. BUT THERE IS A SENSE IN WHICH WE ARE ALL ACTORS PLAYING MANY DIFFERENT ROLES, WITH LIFE ITSELF AS A STAGED PERFORMANCE. OUR DREAMS MAY SHOW US THE STYLIZED AND PUBLIC ASPECTS OF OUR LIVES AS MUCH AS OUR PRIVATE INNER WORLDS, AND DREAMS IN WHICH PERFORMANCE FEATURES COULD WELL BE GIVING US IMPORTANT INFORMATION ABOUT THE TYPES OF ROLES WE ARE ACCUSTOMED TO PLAYING IN DAILY LIFE.

THE WORLD OF STAGE AND SCREEN

Theatrical or film productions are artificial and stylized portrayals of reality. The breakdown of a play into acts and scenes gives it a structure and predictability lacking in normal life; scenery and props are usually pared down to the essentials and actors may speak in a noticeably dramatic way for emphasis, showing and saying only what is essential to get the story or the message across. Films contain a different type of artifice, tricking us into believing that what we see is real by virtue of their detail, or abandoning any pretence at reality altogether in special effects or animation.

When theatre and film appear in our dreams, there are several aspects we need to look at.

Having a dream that features a stage or screen performance can be something of a conundrum – the entertainment is often a fictional scenario played out within the fantasy of the dream, and it can be difficult to tell where one fantasy ends and the other begins. The performers are dream characters one step further removed from reality than usual – what is being highlighted is that they are in a sense not real people even in the dream reality; they are in role, they are not what they seem. Their exaggerated movements and speech may be stressing things that we particularly need to notice. Such exaggerations, together with the fact that the actors are presenting a persona or donning a mask, may also be trying to express how ill at ease

we feel in ourselves, in that we are choosing to project an image rather than being authentic. They may also allow us to take on roles that we ordinarily cannot or will not assume – being a king or tyrant, a jester or fool, a child or even a fantasy figure.

Mime figures may be there to underscore our inability to be heard, although their exaggerated body movements could be telling us that we are more in touch with expressing ourselves physically than verbally.

PERFORMING FOR AN AUDIENCE

Asking yourself how the audience responds could give you insight into why your unconscious is using the performing metaphor. Do they like the performance, or are they chatting among themselves, heckling or walking out? Is the performance an audition? We are constantly being assessed in our daily lives, measured against standards that may be beyond our control, and rewarded in our jobs for "performing" well. It is tempting to measure our self-worth in the light of such standards, and we will work hard towards getting a positive response. In our dreams we may be looking for this response, or may fear being challenged by others when we put ourselves forward. If the audience is ignoring you though, this could be saying something about you not getting a message across or not being noticed. If they are laughing or you are performing badly, it can reveal a fear of failure.

In a dream performance you may forget your lines – losing the thread of why you are performing, or perhaps feeling anxious or over-challenged. It may be that you are being required to say something that goes against the grain, and are having difficulty internalizing it.

CIRCUSES AND CARNIVALS

There is something intriguing about circuses and carnivals. We relish the glitz and glamour, and get an adrenalin rush from watching the daring feats of the high wire. Running away to join the circus is a classic example of escapism, and dreaming of such performances may point to a lack of adventure in our lives – we desire to be part of the show, to become a travelling player and see the world. If you do dream of a circus, look at which roles or acts dominate – the ringmaster, lion-tamer, trapeze artist tightrope-walker, or clown, may provide clues to the issues you are trying to address.

BEING FAMOUS

In our dreams we may dream that we are playing to a packed house, that we are feted as a superstar. This may be because we desire the fame and fortune that stardom brings, or it could represent a desire for attention or recognition of our talents, or a need to be praised just for being who we are. It could also indicate something we long to achieve.

ABOVE Appearing naked in front of a laughing audience is a classic nightmare scenario. Such a dream may be about performance anxiety.
ABOVE LEFT If you have a performance dream, notice if you are a solo player or part of the chorus. Which role suits you best and what does this mean for you?

Be not afeard; the isle is full of noises,
Sounds and sweet airs, that give delight
   and hurt not.
Sometimes a thousand twangling instruments
Will hum about mine ears, and sometime voices
That, if I then had waked after long sleep,
Will make me sleep again: and then, in dreaming,
The clouds me thought would open and
   show riches
Ready to drop upon me that, when I waked,
I cried to dream again.

WILLIAM SHAKESPEARE, THE TEMPEST

CREATIVITY

EXPRESSING OUR CREATIVITY IS A VITAL PART OF THE HUMAN EXPERIENCE AND WE DO THIS IN A MULTITUDE OF WAYS, BOTH ABSTRACT AND LITERAL, THROUGH MEDIA SUCH AS MUSIC, PAINTING, HANDIWORK, POETRY, THEATRE AND DANCE. WE MAY ENGAGE IN THESE PURELY FOR OUR OWN ENJOYMENT OR FOR THE BENEFIT OF OTHERS, FOR AESTHETIC PLEASURE, PERSONAL DEVELOPMENT OR SPIRITUAL REASONS. EVEN PEOPLE WHO REGARD THEMSELVES AS LACKING IN TALENT CAN ENJOY GETTING THEIR HANDS DIRTY, SINGING IN THE SHOWER OR BOPPING TO A CATCHY TUNE. AND WE ALL SHOW TO THE WORLD ASPECTS OF OUR PERSONALITY AND OUR SENSE OF AESTHETICS IN THE CLOTHES WE WEAR AND THE WAY WE DECORATE OUR HOMES.

ABOVE In our dreams there are no restraints on our creativity. We may be able to express ourselves in ways that are not usually available to us.
ABOVE RIGHT The music in our dreams can be warm and inviting or strident and discordant. It may also tell us something about how we express our creativity.

Creative expression may be about entertainment, telling a story or giving a message, but often what we are doing is simply giving an outlet to a mood, or exploring abstract concepts of sound, colour, form or texture.

VISUAL ARTS
In graphic art we are interpreting the world around us and creating a new version that does not exist in reality. In our dreams the reality of an artwork is twice removed from that of our waking life – once by being a graphical representation (on canvas or paper) and again by being a fabrication of our unconscious. The artist may rearrange objects, distort them or place a special focus on particular features. In your dream image, distorted perspective may be an indication of too much emphasis being placed on something. Being out of focus may point to confusion, obscurity or a lack of clarity, while depth or detail in a painting can show an awareness of complexity in your life.

In creating an artwork, there is a significance or value in the subject matter, which is probably key to interpreting your dream. In photography in particular, we may be wanting to take a snapshot of life, to preserve or record something; this may suggest a yearning to hang on to things, to remember, or perhaps to dwell in the past.

In craftwork we add a practical element to creative expression, so if you dream of handcrafted items, you need to look at their function as much as their visual appearance. The presence of such objects may suggest individuality, or a strong personal touch in your environment.

MUSIC
Harmony and discord in music can signpost the same moods in your life – showing whether or not you are at one with your surroundings, your lifestyle, or the people with whom you have regular contact.

Music may be soulful, fun, energetic or restful, romantic or mathematically precise, abstract or lyrical, and these qualities may reflect your moods and feelings. Likewise, different instruments may evoke particular responses in you, or have symbolic value – playing a loud instrument such as a trumpet may enable you to be heard, while drums are used to keep in time or set the pace, and have military associations.

Orchestras, bands and choirs are useful symbols for group behaviour and co-ordination. Depending on the type of group, it may be important to blend in with the crowd, or to let your contribution stand out. Being a soloist or conductor in a dream may be about needing to "go it alone" in some venture, or take responsibility in some way that places you in a spotlight. As a soloist you may feel exposed, but you will also feel the security of having a backing group supporting and adding value to your solo performance.

Practice makes perfect – but going over something again and again can be tedious and stifle your self-expression. In your dreams it may be telling you that you are stuck in a rut or being prevented from doing other things that may be more worthwhile or enjoyable. On the positive side, though, practising is about getting things right; see how the mood of the dream ties in with your life.

CLOTHES AND DÉCOR
The way we dress and decorate our homes says a lot about our personal style – aesthetics, attitudes toward comfort, functionality, culture, prestige and so on. In our dreams and our waking lives alike, we may use colours and styles of dress in a variety of ways; to attract

attention or to blend in, to impress others, to express our sexuality, or to act as camouflage. Our notions of what clothing is appropriate may be quite vague, but appearances count, and we are often judged by them.

BELOW When dreaming of creative pursuits, notice whether the participants enjoy what they are doing or if they are doing it to please someone else. What does the dream say about your creativity?

LEFT An artist is able to interpret the world and create something original. Each night in our dreams we all become artists as we draw on our experiences to create and recreate countless images of ourselves.

COMMUNICATION

HUMANS ARE SOPHISTICATED COMMUNICATORS. WE HAVE EVOLVED NUMEROUS COMPLEX LANGUAGES THAT WE CAN USE TO EXPRESS THE MOST DETAILED NUANCES OF OUR FEELINGS AND EXPERIENCES. WE HAVE DEVELOPED INGENIOUS SYSTEMS OF RECORDING INFORMATION AND TRANSMITTING IT ACROSS TIME AND DISTANCE. WE ALSO COMMUNICATE WITHOUT WORDS — BODY LANGUAGE AND TONE OF VOICE SOMETIMES GIVING MORE INFORMATION THAN WHAT WE UTTER. DESPITE THIS, OR PERHAPS BECAUSE OF THE COMPLEXITY OF OUR AVAILABLE COMMUNICATION CHANNELS, WE ARE OFTEN FRUSTRATED BY MISCOMMUNICATION, A LACK OF INFORMATION, OR BY CONFUSION OVER MIXED MESSAGES.

In trying to decipher our dreams of communication, we need to pay attention to what is being said, who is saying it and in what way, as well as to what is happening at the same time. Are people shouting or whispering? Are they looking at us? Do we understand them? Is what they say compatible with what they are doing? Also consider whether the communication is happening face to face or at a distance.

BELOW Shouting in a dream can indicate that you need to speak up for yourself. Does it feel as though no one is listening to you, or that in order to make yourself heard you have to raise your voice?

SPEAKING WITH A PURPOSE

To give information and express our feelings and opinions are probably the most important reasons we communicate. But we also speak and write to change or manipulate others – to persuade them round to our point of view, by preaching or dictating to them or by using our expressions to intimidate them. We may feel uncomfortable with silence, and feel we need to fill the void with chatter to hide or deny our insecurity. And of course we talk for the pleasure of it – to make or maintain contact, or to entertain.

Get a feel for the purpose of the communication in the dream and relate it to how others speak to you in real life, as well as how you use communication yourself.

If your communication is not straightforward in the dream, try to understand why this is – perhaps you don't trust that others will accept you or agree with you if you say what you mean. If this is the case, it could be worth looking at your beliefs and checking if they are still true for you so that you can feel more confident in them or dispense with them.

LANGUAGE

We often use our dreams to try to decipher situations we don't understand, and may use language as a metaphor for our confusion – indistinct speech, riddles or foreign tongues, for example. There may be clues in the dream to why we are not communicating effectively or

---

COMMUNICATION DREAM

"I was at a noisy party where everyone was talking at the same time. I couldn't understand what anyone was saying – but I realized I could understand what they were thinking. They were thinking really rude thoughts, criticising each other's clothes, making personal comments. But their words were all jumbled as they came out. I was too embarrassed to say anything and I wanted to run out. I was afraid that someone else could understand my own thoughts – namely, that they were all animals. I woke up feeling completely lost and disoriented.

I am quite perceptive about what is going on with others, but don't always trust my intuitions and get confused by lies and subterfuge. I have also always had a problem saying what I mean and this dream was showing me my fears and frustrations around this – often I just keep quiet when I am angry with someone and really feel like being very rude."

BELOW What would a child shouting mean in your dreams? Could it be that you are afraid to say what you think for fear of being judged as childish or rude? Or perhaps you have a child who is struggling to be heard?

LEFT We adapt the way we communicate to fit with the situation. Talking to our work colleagues is different from talking to close friends or family. How you communicate tells you a lot about how you relate to other people.

RIGHT Pay attention to body language and subtle signals as well as what is being said. Looking away while someone is talking to you could mean many different things.

understanding others, and it could be useful to see if you are in contact with people in your daily life who are hard to fathom, or who are not what they seem.

RIGHT Children love to whisper and share their secrets. Is there something private that you would like to say to someone? What is holding you back?

SELF-EXPRESSION

In our dreams, we may be involved in the communication process or perhaps we are onlookers seeing others interact. Watching ourselves talking can be very revealing. Are we at ease talking? Or do we find it difficult in the dream? Are we happy with what we are saying or are the words stilted and awkward? If we can't see ourselves but we are still part of the dream how do we interpret what people are saying to us? The whole secret to good

or accurate dream interpretation is asking questions: why are we saying this? Who are we talking to? What is their response?

SHOUTING

We cry out to make others hear, or express intensity. It is not uncommon, especially among children, to dream of shouting at the top of your voice but barely a whisper comes out. This is almost certainly to do with feeling you are not heard, that your voice doesn't count.

The meaning of every dream is the fulfilment of a wish.

SIGMUND FREUD

ENERGY AND POWER

ENERGY TAKES A MULTITUDE OF FORMS, AND IN OUR DREAMS WE ENCOUNTER IT IN THE CATACLYSMIC ERUPTIONS OF NATURE – VOLCANOES, LIGHTNING, EARTHQUAKES – AS MUCH AS IN OURSELVES. THOUGH WE CAN EXPRESS OUR ENERGY POSITIVELY THROUGH DANCE, SPORT AND VERY MANY OTHER ACTIVITIES, IT IS OFTEN CHANNELLED INTO AGGRESSION AND VIOLENCE. LEARNING HOW TO CHANNEL VIOLENT, AGGRESSIVE ENERGY CAN BE A LIFELONG STRUGGLE AND WE MAY NEVER FEEL TOTALLY CONFIDENT THAT WE HAVE IT UNDER OUR CONTROL. THE TRICK IS TO ALLOW THE FEELINGS WITHOUT ACTING THEM OUT. IF WE SUPPRESS THEM AND TURN THEM IN ON OURSELVES, WE WILL DO OURSELVES HARM.

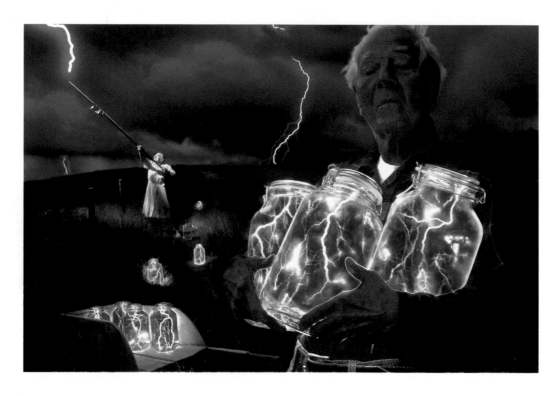

ABOVE The universe is born out of energy and our powerful responses may be much more natural than we think. To dream of nature's forces may mean that you have personal power issues to work out. How do others see you?

VIOLENT ORIGINS

Stars are born out of cosmic explosions on an unimaginable scale. Fiery forces deep within our own planet erupt as volcanoes so destructive that they can engulf entire cities and set up far-reaching tidal waves. Our entire universe was created in violent energy reactions, and continues to evolve and be transformed in this way. Even our own birth is an energetic and sometimes violent moment, a dramatic experience for mother and child alike, and the baby's first gasp of breath is a struggle.

It is not surprising, then, that we may be troubled when such images occur in our dreams. It is as though we are struggling with the violence inherent in our existence, and trying to reconcile this with the passivity and control that are in many ways esteemed in our society.

VIOLENCE CURTAILED

The struggle with energy and violence is so instinctive that it permeates our unconscious, but there are precious few socially sanctioned outlets for this in our normal waking lives. Being civilized, controlled, elegant, and sophisticated are prized at the expense of emotional expression. We still have the same instinctive

reactions and negative emotions as our primitive forebears, but the "fight or flight" response is often not appropriate in our modern world. We are not allowed to be violent, no matter how incensed we are, and if we do become violent or if we have temper tantrums, we are punished, and we may feel overwhelmed, frightened and guilty at the very thought of it.

We need these dreams as safety valves for our unexpressed violence, anger and frustration, and to give us an opportunity to find alternative ways of dealing with the world so that these feelings don't well up in the first place. Sometimes our unconscious presents us with dreams of energy or violence in its raw and awesome state in order to forge a safe link between our calm outer persona and our turbulent inner self, between our civilized, rational exterior and the anger and passions that many of us tend to bottle up. In this way, having violent dreams can be a healthy experience.

The more elaborate, complex and impenetrable the mask of sophistication a person wears, the bigger the gap between feeling and response. Conversely, the more instinctual and expressive the person, the less likely they are to be troubled by such dreams, as they have already found ways of venting their energy safely in waking life.

ATTACK AND DEFENCE

If violence is a real part of your life, you may be constantly in fear and on your guard against being attacked. The trauma of even a single attack may linger for years. It can prompt feelings of anger and violence, and you may want to act these out on particular individuals. However, the feelings may be unfocused and you are simply searching for a target for them. But if you are powerless to act on your feelings in real life, you may well have these encounters in your dreams instead. You can also actively use your dreams to deal with violence in a positive way – it can be beneficial to replay the scene of an attack in your dreams in such a way that you successfully defend yourself. This can give you the strength and feeling of self-worth you need to move on.

The physical attacks of your dreams can be metaphors for many other ways in which you might be attacked. Perhaps your ideas or actions have been harshly criticized and you take this personally, or you have to bear the brunt of someone else's anger, even when you haven't deserved it. In these cases it is useful to look at the role you play – are you aggressive, taunting, or an innocent bystander, a victim of circumstances? How you respond to an attack is also important, and your dream could give you clues as to how to deal with aggression in others.

LEFT We may think ourselves cool and calm, yet our dreams may show what is bubbling beneath the surface, like a volcano waiting to erupt.
MIDDLE LEFT The tighter the grip on our natural responses, the more likely we are to "blow up".
BOTTOM LEFT Cosmic explosions are what sets the universe in motion. Powerful, violent energy is part of life – we can use this force to create or to destroy – it's up to us.

ENERGY DREAM

"I could see worlds in collision, entire galaxies erupting in fireballs and glorious colourful explosions. It was staggering, mind-blowing, and I could see how the world was made out of conflagration. It seems strange that such violent destruction can result in so much beauty.

I think that my dream was trying to tell me that I had to put more energy, more passion, into making things happen, that I had to get rid of the apathy that was holding me back."

LIVING IN THE WORLD

From the moment of our birth until we die we build up a wealth of experiences through our interactions with the "world out there". These experiences shape who we are and guide our behaviour. How we feel, how we express ourselves, how we react with the world and the people in it, combine to produce a unique experience for each of us. Often we peg our self-worth on external factors, such as our level of wealth, or our achievements or social status, and we expend a great deal of time and energy trying to gain more of these things. Our aspirations become preoccupations and we try to work out aspects of these things in our dreams. In comparing ourselves with others, we may set ourselves up for competition and conflict. But sometimes the world delivers experiences over which we have little or no control – change is part of life and accidents can happen – and our dreams can help us adjust and warn us of potential trouble.

AMBITIONS AND GOALS

WE ALL HAVE OUR AMBITIONS AND GOALS, HOPES AND DESIRES, AND ENJOY THE SATISFACTION OF SUCCESS WHEN WE FULFIL THEM OR DISAPPOINTMENT WHEN WE CANNOT. BUT IF WE GET TO A POINT AT WHICH WE ARE CONSUMED BY UNFULFILLED AMBITIONS, OUR UNCONSCIOUS WILL TRY TO WORK WITH THEM IN OUR DREAMS, TO SEE A WAY FORWARD OR TO ACCEPT SOMETHING DIFFERENT FOR US. IF WE FAIL TO ACHIEVE SOMETHING THAT IS REALLY IMPORTANT FOR US OR TURN OUR BACK ON A BURNING AMBITION, OUR UNCONSCIOUS WILL PRODUCE DREAMS THAT MAKE US FOCUS ON THAT GOAL AND FIND A WAY TO MAKE US SUCCEED.

REACH FOR THE SKY

We don't have to put a limit on our hopes and aspirations. If we aim for something in our dreams that we have no hope of actually achieving, it may not matter that our ambitions are unrealistic. Such fantasies can be liberating – they give us scope to stretch our self-imposed limitations, and to make possible things that might otherwise seem far-fetched.

BELOW A lock and key is a powerful symbol. Do you have an unfulfilled ambition locked away inside of you, and if so, what is the key to realizing it? Perhaps the key is just out of reach, or maybe it doesn't quite fit the lock.

If an ambition remains out of reach because we have aimed too high, however, it can cause distress. It may leave us feeling that we will never achieve what we want and make us feel like giving up. In which case we may need to take a closer look at it, at the symbolic value of what we are failing to achieve. In asking questions about a dream symbol we may find out why we are being so unrealistic and aiming too high. We can gain more insight into what makes us set ourselves up for failure and find ways to set ourselves more realistic targets.

STUMBLING BLOCKS

There may well be valid reasons for not achieving an ambition – perhaps deep down inside you know that achieving it may not be as beneficial as you might like. For example, you may have been offered a fantastic job that will mean moving abroad, but because it offers you things you really want you may well be blinded to the attendant

BELOW To dream that you are doing a tedious, repetitive task may suggest that your goals are set too low. Perhaps it's time to get your ideas in order, rather like the bottles on the assembly line, and review your ambitions.

disadvantages or dangers – your family doesn't want to go, your parents would miss you, the company is not as stable as you want to believe, or your expertise isn't up to a high-powered job.

These unconscious realizations may manifest themselves as something stopping us in our dreams. This could be a locked door or a fence that stops us going along a certain path. A guard is another common symbol; this is usually someone impassive, anonymous and immovable who bars our way. If we don't find a way past the obstacles in our dream, then perhaps we ought to reconsider our ambition. But if we do manage to get through, this may give us a clue as to what our best course of action should be. We can relate it to our waking lives and find a way of achieving our goals and ambitions. On the other hand it may show us that although achieving our goal is possible, it is going to be very difficult, so perhaps it would be better to scale back or drop what it is that we are after.

SYMBOLIC IMAGERY
Literal images of goals and targets may appear in our dream to symbolize our personal ambitions. Games involving scoring goals, or aiming accurately for a small target, such as golf or darts, can show us how focused we are and whether or not our ambitions are fixed or keep changing. As well as looking at the nature of the

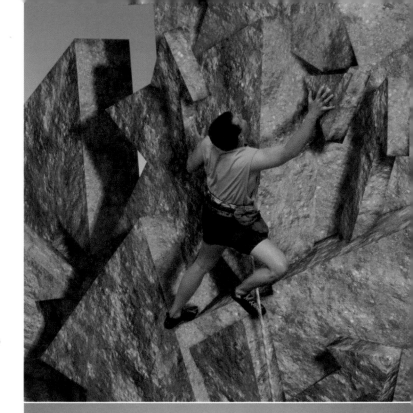

RIGHT Some ambitions are not easy to achieve but require great skill and tenacity if we are to make it to the top.
MIDDLE RIGHT A dream could suggest that achieving your goal will require total commitment, just like an athlete preparing to race.
BOTTOM RIGHT Our dreams may tell us to take control and put ourselves forward, rather than sitting in the background waiting to be asked.

goal, notice whether the game in your dream is a team effort, and if so who is helping or opposing you, or whether you are solely responsible in some way.

THE SCALE OF OUR AMBITIONS
Remember that our goals may be anything from major lifelong ambitions to relatively trivial targets, such as tidying up a messy cupboard, so if the dream does appear obviously to be about goals or ambitions but you are unable to see immediately what it could be referring to, think laterally about the nature of what you might be trying to process. Even small goals may take on greater significance than they deserve if they link into personal hang-ups – if your mother was always pestering you to tidy your room when you were a child, for instance, you may feel obsessed, angry or resistant about tidying up. Being goal oriented may also mean that you will tend to turn ordinary activities into goals, into something you can check off a list, rather than just being a regular part of daily life.

Dreams are a dress rehearsal for life. ALFRED ADLER

ACHIEVEMENT AND SUCCESS

FROM THE MOMENT WE TAKE OUR FIRST BREATH, WE ARE DRIVEN TO ACHIEVE. FOR INFANTS, LEARNING TO EAT, CRAWL, STAND UP, WALK AND SPEAK IS A MATTER OF SURVIVAL, AND OUR NATURAL INSTINCT TO ACHIEVE THESE THINGS IS SUPPORTED BY PARENTAL ENCOURAGEMENT. AS WE GROW UP, OUR ACHIEVEMENTS BECOME MORE COMPLEX AND THE WAY WE MEASURE SUCCESS CHANGES. AT SCHOOL AND COLLEGE WE ARE ENCOURAGED TO SUCCEED ACADEMICALLY AND WHEN WE ENTER THE WORLD OF WORK, ACHIEVEMENT IS LINKED WITH JOB SATISFACTION. OUR DREAMS CAN SHOW US WHERE WE FEEL PROUD OF OUR ACHIEVEMENTS AND POINT TO AREAS WHERE WE FEEL DISSATISFIED AND UNFULFILLED.

MAKING IT

You may dream of winning an award or prize of some sort to mark your achievement. Or perhaps someone claps you on the back and says "well done". You may dream that you score a goal or play the winning hand or captain your favourite team, or that you suddenly have acquired a new skill, such as being able to play the violin. Maybe you have suddenly become famous and are signing autographs and giving

BELOW What would a running child mean in your dreams? Are you still that racing child eager for success or do you have some growing up to do before you make it?

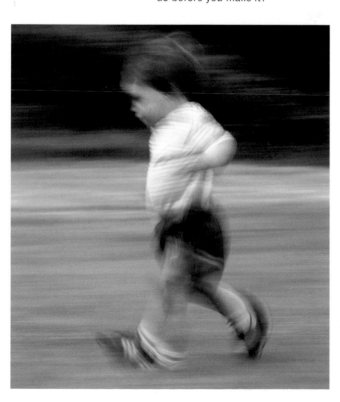

press conferences. Your dream may even give you a halo, a set of wings, a new power such as flying or walking on water. Such dreams could suggest that you are proud of your achievements. Alternatively, they may point up a glaring mis-match between your dream self and your actual experience. Perhaps you need to define what "making it" would mean for you and find an arena in which to express yourself.

SUCCESS IN OTHERS

In your dream, it may even be someone else and not you who is successful. Consider how you feel towards this person. You may feel warm and supportive and full of encouragement or you may feel jealous and competitive. But it is also worth bearing in mind that the other people in our dreams may also actually be displacements of ourselves.

Dreaming of someone else's success could be as close as we can get to admitting our own success, to being told we've done well and to knowing that we're alright. If you know the person who is successful in your dream, try to understand what they represent to you, and see what it is about their character or what they are doing that makes things go well. This may show you how you can be more successful.

TEAM EFFORT

Sometimes we dream of the success of a group – our favourite football team winning the cup or scoring lots of goals, a country finally negotiating peace after being at war for many years, or the company we work for expanding so we get that pay rise we wanted. In this kind of scenario, the group effort may be key to understanding the meaning of your dream – perhaps it is a hint not to try to do everything yourself if you want to achieve your goals, or to enable you to place some trust in the people who may help you on your way.

ACKNOWLEDGEMENT

Part of our drive for success is rooted in our desire to be acknowledged, and to be noticed and admired. Dreams of parents, friends and partners watching and cheering you on may demonstrate that you feel valued as a person, while being feted by the public, such as being cheered by a crowd or carried on their shoulders, may show a desire for public recognition. Perhaps you would like the world to see and acknowledge your status and everything that you have achieved. Prizes and medals may indicate that you need a constant reminder of your successes, and

RIGHT A silver cup is a symbol that most of us associate with successful achievement. Seeing it in a dream may mean we would like to win a prize for something that we feel proud of doing.

ABOVE How does it feel to be successful? Life's peak moments can pass us by in a blur because we are so caught up with speed and wanting to win.

that you are not able to rely on your own awareness of your abilities to realize what you are worth. The appearance of any of these things does, however, mean that you know within yourself that you are worthwhile and that you deserve some level of recognition.

LEFT College graduation is typically marked by fun and celebration in honour of our achievements. For many people this moment represents the fulfilment of a childhood wish.

DREAM OF SUCCESS

"I was riding in a limousine along a street lined with cheering fans; as it was a convertible, they could get really close. I looked really cool and well dressed. All these people were cheering and whistling as if I had done something really amazing. I didn't know what I had done, but it felt really good! When I woke up I thought it would be cool to be recognized like that, and since then I've been sending demos off to radio stations and record companies. I don't know if I'll get anywhere, but it feels worthwhile – if I have any moments of doubt I just have to remember that dream to spur me on. I can't wait for it to be real, to be cheered by real fans."

RIGHT When can we say we have finally reached the summit? Even in our dreams it may be difficult to plot such an exact moment, although there are times in everyone's life when we should feel proud of ourselves. When did you last feel on top of the world?

BELOW It is not always easy to measure our achievements and we may feel the need for some kind of external validation, such as more money or a certificate, to increase our self-esteem.

JOBS AND WORK

WE SPEND A LOT OF TIME AT WORK, AND EARNING A LIVING IN A SATISFYING WAY IS ONE OF LIFE'S GREATEST CHALLENGES. IT IS ONLY NATURAL FOR WORK TO OCCUPY AN IMPORTANT PART OF OUR DREAM LIFE. BUT WORK IN A DREAM IS NOT ALWAYS ABOUT AN ACTIVITY THAT WE DO — WE ENCOUNTER PEOPLE WHO ARE OPERATING IN THEIR WORK ROLES ALL THE TIME, AND OUR COLLEAGUES MAY ALSO FIGURE PROMINENTLY. ENJOYING OUR WORK MAY BE REFLECTED IN POSITIVE, HAPPY DREAMS ABOUT IT, OR DREAMS IN WHICH WE GRAPPLE WITH INTERESTING REAL-LIFE PROBLEMS THAT WE CAN'T BEAR TO LET GO OF EVEN IN OUR SLEEP. SOMETIMES STRESS AND ANXIETY RELATED TO WORK WILL ALSO SURFACE.

ABOVE When work seems like drudgery, it could be time to review your career options.
ABOVE RIGHT Your dreams may reflect what it is you really want to do with your life.
ABOVE FAR RIGHT You might dream about the work of others rather than yourself. Is this a reflection of someone in your life who has authority over you? Is the authority justified or does it worry and frustrate you?

WORK AND EMOTIONS
Unfortunately, for many people work means stress, boredom, frustration, unhappiness, and anger; we may feel unchallenged or abused or taken for granted, and our dreams may well reflect such feelings. We may say or do something extreme in the work environment of our dream, and wake worrying that we might act out such stuff in real life. But the point of these dreams may in fact be to address just that possibility – to let off steam in the safety of our dreams so that we don't cause a scene at work.

Work dreams may seem fairly realistic, but at other times our unconscious will create a memorable scenario to draw our attention to what is bothering us.

Dreaming of work might also be symbolic of more general issues, such as survival or money, how to rise to a challenge or deal with pressure, feelings of inadequacy, subservience or anger and a myriad other experiences.

PEOPLE AT WORK
We do not always dream about our own jobs, however. As in our daily lives, we are constantly in contact with or seeing images of others as they go about their work, from shopkeepers to bank managers, newsreaders to teachers, factory workers to artists and chefs. We probably hold countless attitudes about those roles – wishing we could be in the other person's shoes, or thanking our lucky stars that we

aren't. We may admire people for their work, thinking that they must be clever or talented or courageous to do what they do, and envy the satisfaction or prestige or fame that goes with their wonderful-looking jobs. Or perhaps we hate the idea of the tedium or lack of status of a particular job, the confinement of an office or the uncertainty of contract work.

Engaging with strangers in our dreams may often be in the context of their occupation, and our attitude to that occupation. Teachers, bosses and policemen, for instance, tend to be authority figures, and your experiences in real life will be crucial in forming your attitude to such figures. As a child, did you have teachers who picked on you, inflicted corporal punishment or made you feel stupid? Or did they inspire you, understand and encourage you, satisfy and nurture your curiosity or give you a love of reading?

People at work can symbolize many different things. To dream of a cleaner, for instance, may indicate you need to get your house in order and to "clean up", while an accountant might suggest that you take stock of your affairs and get organized. An artist on the other hand may suggest that you need to relax your attitudes and think laterally or engage more with your intuitive, creative side.

COLLEAGUES

We spend much of our waking lives with colleagues, so it is not surprising if we dream about them. Often their function in our dreams will be similar to that of friends, in that they will appear because they have particular characteristics that we need to address. But in many cases their role will be more important – bosses in particular may bring up important issues relating to authority, power and status.

RIGHT Some workplaces are big and imposing. Dreaming that you are in such a building can make you feel small and insignificant, especially if you are alone.
MIDDLE RIGHT Sometimes it feels as though you are just going round and round and not getting anywhere. Your dream may be showing you that progress does not always follow a straight line.
BOTTOM RIGHT Repetitive work is not necessarily boring. Your dream may be a reminder to take a pride in all your endeavours and know that every job has its part to play.

WORKPLACES AND RESOURCES

If you find in your dream that you are unable to do things because the equipment you have for doing your job is inadequate or the work environment is unpleasant, it could be saying something general about your material wellbeing or your ability to get things done.

Do you feel that you get what you want out of life, or that there are constantly obstacles to what you want to do? Our physical environment can have a major impact on our emotional state, so it is worth noting how you feel about the workplace of your dream as much as what you are doing or the people you are with.

WORK DREAM

"I was due to go on my first business trip, to the headquarters of a major bank. In my dream I arrived at their imposing building and went up in the lift. The doors opened directly into the boardroom, which contained a massive table surrounded by middle-aged men in suits. As they looked up I realized to my horror that, although I was wearing a smart black jacket and smart black shoes, I was also wearing a frilly, homemade nightdress.

This dream was clearly to do with not feeling confident in myself or comfortable in the imposing and masculine setting of the bank. I was afraid that I couldn't pull off the meeting successfully, that I would somehow make a serious gaffe, be intimidated or not be taken seriously."

SPORTS AND GAMES

FUN, PHYSICAL WELLBEING AND A SENSE OF ACHIEVEMENT ARE JUST SOME OF THE REASONS WE TAKE PART IN SPORTS AND GAMES. THEY ALSO PROVIDE A WAY OF ENGAGING WITH OTHER PEOPLE IN A VERY ACTIVE WAY, AS BOTH TEAM MEMBERS AND OPPONENTS, AS WELL AS HELPING US RELEASE STRESS AND CHANNEL OUR AGGRESSIVE IMPULSES. FOR ARMCHAIR SPORTSMEN OR TEAM SUPPORTERS AT SPORTS FIXTURES, THERE IS THE EXCITEMENT AND CAMARADERIE OF WATCHING A FAVOURITE TEAM OR FAVOURITE SPORT IN ACTION. WITH THESE DREAMS, WE NEED TO ASK OURSELVES ABOUT THE SPORT WE ARE ENGAGED IN, HOW WE PLAY, AND OUR MOTIVATIONS AND FEELINGS, AS WELL AS WHAT ACTUALLY HAPPENS.

GAMES PEOPLE PLAY

The various forms of sporting and leisure activities represent many qualities. For instance, a violent rugby match may have more to do with aggression and teamwork than the leisurely, non-contact style of a round of golf, while an intellectually absorbing chess game is mainly concerned with strategy and has almost nothing to do with physicality. There are also many games that we play simply for fun, such as beach volleyball or the role-playing games of a child's make-believe world where the rules are made up as they go along.

SUBLIMATION OF AGGRESSION

For many people, sports and games provide a much-needed way of working through aggression and frustration. The positive effects of strenuous physical activity on the emotions are well documented, and in some sports, hitting or kicking a ball can be a great substitute for doing the same to someone who has made you very angry! By analysing how we feel and how we are behaving and reacting to others in our dream, we can try to uncover the real cause of our aggressive feelings and work through them or lay them to rest.

OPPONENTS

Who are you playing with and against in your dream? Your opponents may be real people, they may represent abstract qualities – luck, fate, challenges, opposition – or they may be an aspect of yourself that you are at odds with.

Often opponents will be people with whom we are having some kind of power struggle or conflict. Who wins is often a vital question, as it could indicate what is actually happening in an important relationship, what you wish for or what you fear. Look at how seriously you take the game – you may want simply to put your opponent in their place, to hurt them badly, or even to eliminate them altogether.

TEAMS

Being part of a team gives a great sense of belonging, going beyond our individual needs to unite in a common goal. Teams give us a place, a role, a bond with others. They show us who our friends are and how much we rely on others to achieve our goals. Sports teams can also be a

BELOW What sport are you pursuing in your dream? Is it something that you normally do? **BELOW RIGHT** What are the items of equipment associated with a game or sport? Perhaps these have a significance in your dream. **BELOW FAR RIGHT** Dreams of running a race may raise issues of winning and losing in your life.

RIGHT Dreams of top sports people are fairly common. Such dreams may represent a wish-fulfilment, an ambition to be the "best" at something, or to be famous and admired. What could this mean for you?

metaphor for other social groups in our lives, such as the family or work team, and looking at how they pull together and the roles people play may be significant in relation to these units.

COMPETITION AND RESULTS

Competition is an all-pervasive feature of our society, and the games we play are often about proving who is best, who has the greatest talent, skill or intellectual ability. For many people, getting ahead gives a feeling of self-worth that they may otherwise be not capable of feeling. Winning or losing a dream game could be crucial to how you see yourself – your confidence or assertiveness, what your role is in relation to your opponent or your team, or how you view your skills and talents. If you have a relationship

where you are constantly racking up points against each other, this may show up in your dreams as a competition of some sort.

PLAYING THE GAME

Cheating or rule-breaking may hint at an unfair situation in your life, or one in which someone is being underhand with you. Rules may be about social restrictions, so check whether you know what the rules of the game are, and whether it is you or someone else who is breaking them.

COMPETITIVE DREAM

"I was playing chess against my father, using life-sized pieces. Although we laughed and joked as we played, I knew we were playing for big stakes and this created an underlying seriousness, a feeling of menace that affected my game. Behind the laughter I was in crisis: I wanted to win so badly it hurt, and I wanted to hurt him, even kill him, by winning. This was a very powerful dream and it made me realize that I had a lot to work out about my relationship with my father. We have always been competitive, and he is also very pushy, expecting me to do well, earn well, and drive myself as hard as he does. I've always felt I have a lot to live up to and although I don't like it, I've always done what he wants. In this dream I realized that I didn't have to be dominated by him forever, but that I would need to be more assertive for that to happen."

LEFT Every sport has its own set of rules and we need to understand them before we can enjoy the game. Are you a player or a spectator in your dream?
FAR LEFT Very physical team sports can be a good way of letting off steam. Being part of a team in your dream is a sign of belonging, or wanting to belong.

MONEY

WHAT DOES MONEY REPRESENT TO YOU? WHEN IT COMES TO WORKING WITH OUR DREAMS THE ANSWER TO THIS IS
CRUCIAL. MOST PEOPLE WILL ACKNOWLEDGE THAT THEY WANT IT, AND ALMOST CERTAINLY THAT THEY NEED IT, BUT BEYOND
THAT OUR RESPONSES CAN DIFFER MARKEDLY FROM PERSON TO PERSON. PERHAPS YOU SEE IT AS A MEANS TO AN END, OR
AN END IN ITSELF; MAYBE YOU THINK THAT IT REPRESENTS FREEDOM AND CAN LIBERATE PEOPLE, OR YOU MIGHT SEE IT AS AN
ENSLAVER. OUR OWN AND OTHERS' ATTITUDES TO MONEY IN REAL LIFE WILL INEVITABLY BE REFLECTED IN OUR DREAMS;
HOW MUCH THERE IS, WHERE IT CAME FROM AND WHAT WE DO WITH IT WILL ALSO BE SIGNIFICANT.

ASSOCIATIONS

Money is generally said to point to opportunity and reward or power. Some associate it with relationships, so in this way receiving it is linked to the birth of a child, finding it could suggest benefiting from a prosperous marriage, and wasting or losing it may mean that you are wasting your love on someone unworthy.

Using a Freudian model, hoarding money implies anal fixation. Money can also be used to represent resources in general. Bear in mind that it could be denoting riches in terms of time, energy, knowledge, love and so on, rather than material or monetary wealth. Consider your relationship with these other resources too and think about how rich or poor you feel.

Some of these money associations may make sense to you and help you to understand what your dream is really about. If not, you will need to dig a bit deeper, and really try to understand what money means to you on a much more personal basis, and thus what it symbolizes in your dream.

BELOW Think about what money may symbolize to you. Love? Security? Status? Freedom? Success? It is important to understand your own reactions before you interpret your dreams on the subject.

WHAT MONEY CAN BUY

It is what we can have and do with money – as well as what is unavailable to us if we don't have it – that gives it much of its value. We may feel that it gives us the freedom to have the things we want, including leisure time and opportunities to see and do things that aren't free. But having acquired wealth, we may feel burdened by our possessions and afraid of losing them, and we may also feel trapped by the need to carry on generating it.

Dreams of money may be simple wish fulfilment, or we may find they show us how to get it, the frustrations of not having it, or the fear of being suddenly deprived of it. But we can also use money dreams as a more general symbol for greed and materialism, opportunity, the loss of something we value, or even of being trapped.

STATUS AND POWER

Money can convey power and status. We can add to this the idea that money is a reward, so having or not having it differentiates us further and makes us feel more or less worthwhile as people. These issues may well bother us, keying in to our inherent sense of self-worth, and dreams of money – especially in relation to a salary or wage – can be about this idea of our value, of how much we are being appreciated.

GIVE AND TAKE

If you are hoarding or counting money in your dream, you may be afraid that it will run out or be feeling insecure; similarly putting

---

MONEY DREAM

"I was being asked to pay admission to the cinema. I had brought a single coin in my pocket, but couldn't find it anywhere – it had slipped through a hole. A terrible grief washed over me. I couldn't understand why it should pain me so much – it was only a trip to the cinema after all.

This dream was about having given up a successful career in film-making to devote myself to my family. My children were growing up and needed me less and less, and I was aware that in the meantime my precious career seemed lost. Although I didn't regret having had children, I was experiencing pain at having let my career slip through my fingers."

---

it in the bank may be to do with security. Holding on to money can also represent holding on to ideas, rather than putting them into action. If you are giving money away, do you do so with a spirit of generosity, or because you simply want to get rid of it? Spending or giving money freely can imply a certain faith or trust in things working out, that your own needs will always be met, and this can be tremendously reassuring if you normally worry about such matters.

Owing or being owed money in a dream could be a worry about literally being burdened by debt. Looked at in a broader sense though, ask yourself if you are concerned about being indebted to someone in a more general way – perhaps they have done you a favour or you feel guilty about asking for help. You may also feel taken advantage of.

TYPES OF MONEY

The form the money takes in your dreams may hold another layer of significance. Cash is readily available, and whether it

---

comes in the shape of coins or notes may indicate how much you value whatever it represents to you. An IOU or cheque may signify indebtedness, delayed gratification or uncertainty around whether you will be repaid; gift vouchers may suggest generosity, but may also hint that whatever they represent has some specific value or limitation placed on it. If you dream of foreign money it could be that you are unsure of the value of something.

ABOVE Do you associate money with particular people in your life?
ABOVE LEFT If you dream of gambling in association with money perhaps you are feeling financially insecure?
ABOVE FAR LEFT To dream about saving will mean different things to different people.

BELOW Precious gold nuggets and ingots symbolize great wealth. If they appear in a dream look at the context to see what they mean.

AUTHORITY AND DISCIPLINE

WHEN WE ARE CHILDREN OUR PARENTS AND TEACHERS TELL US WHAT WE CAN AND CAN'T DO. OFTEN THE AIM OF THIS IS TO TEACH US SOCIAL NORMS OR PREVENT US FROM HURTING OURSELVES. BUT MUCH OF THE AUTHORITY THAT ADULTS WIELD OVER CHILDREN IS TO DO WITH THEIR OWN INTERESTS – PROTECTING THEIR BELONGINGS, THEIR NEEDS, THEIR FEELINGS. AS ADULTS WE MIGHT ASSOCIATE PUNISHMENT WITH AN ELEMENT OF UNFAIRNESS AND IMPOSITION, OR WE MIGHT SEE IT AS SOMETHING WE DESERVE MORE OF. AUTHORITY FIGURES MIGHT BE SEEN AS UNJUST AND REPRESSIVE, BUT WE MAY ALSO PRODUCE THEM IN OUR DREAMS AS A SYMBOL OF SECURITY, OR OF WISDOM AND GUIDANCE.

In punishing a child the stated aim may be to teach the child what is safe or dangerous, right and wrong, and acceptable or unacceptable, but from time to time, punishment may be meted out that has nothing to do with a child having done something "bad", but rather with an adult venting frustration or simply being a bully, and this can be frightening and perplexing.

INNER DISCIPLINE

When we grow up our attitude to authority and punishment can be quite complex, so we may use dream time to unravel how we feel, especially if we come up against problematic authority figures, moral dilemmas or confusion in our daily lives. As adults, there usually isn't the same sort of immediate authority

figure standing over us like when we were children. Hopefully we will have developed an innate sense of what is right and wrong; we have a greater understanding of the consequences of our actions and are able to exercise our own judgement and discretion. Laws and the fear of punishment keep most of us in check where our self-discipline or morality may otherwise slip.

Over the course of our lives, our unconscious takes note of the countless rules and injunctions laid down in our early years by parents, teachers and prefects; as we grow older we become aware of other authority figures and bodies of law, and we notice how others respond to these as well. We also develop subtle ways of avoiding punishment and guilt. If we are acting in a way our

unconscious thinks doesn't suit our own interests, it will let us know through the symbolism of our dreams by creating a figure who can tell us how to behave.

PUNISHMENT

Our experience of punishment and how we respond to it is also a personal one. Being given detention at school may have been immensely shameful and humiliating for one person, but for another merely irritating or even a fairly normal occurrence. Indeed for some, being punished by "the establishment" establishes "street cred". In some societies beating a child for a wrongdoing may be considered a normal – even essential – part of their growing up, whereas in others it is anathema, and thought to be damaging. So to understand what

BELOW RIGHT As children we soon learn who is in charge and this may be reflected in our dreams. Who was the dominant authority figure when you were growing up?
BELOW How we respond to authority in any of its smallest forms is very revealing. Even a red traffic light can trigger issues around sticking to or breaking the rules.

RIGHT Laws and the fear of being punished keep most of us in check. This can make us feel that we are under surveillance or living in a police state, and may show up in our dreams. Who is watching you?

punishment means in your dreams may mean coming to terms with how you view it in real life. Does it make you feel angry, guilty, submissive or humiliated, or does withstanding it give you strength? Did you feel you deserved it? If you are meting it out, look hard at what you were feeling and who you are punishing. Note what the punishment is, how severe it is, and if you feel it is deserved. Also try to discover why it is being meted out, and what it achieves.

REBELLING

What if you don't want to be told what to do, or you believe that an authority figure is wrong or evil, or you feel that someone is acting in an authoritarian way towards you but shouldn't? If your boss tells you to forge a signature or your partner dominates or controls your relationship, you may well feel resentful but unable to be assertive or to inject a reasonable balance. If you can't deal with the matter in an adult way, you may represent the dominant person in your dreams as a teacher or parent. Your powerlessness may reduce you to a small child or even animal, or your resentment may manifest in your dreams as a symbolic rebellion or mutiny.

AUTHORITY FIGURES

The area of our lives in which we are having difficulties, together with our upbringing, social standing, beliefs and cultural background, will determine who the authority figure in our dream will be. It may be a police officer if we are in danger of breaking the law, or a priest if religious or moral principles are at stake. For others it might be a judge, lawyer, traffic warden, headteacher, monarch, even a god. Each of these represents something different, and we need to look at what they mean to us to find out what their presence in our dream means.

AUTHORITY DREAM

"In my dream I couldn't find my car keys, and realized my wife had hidden them. I asked her for them back but she said no, it wasn't my turn to drive the car. She told me to go and stand in the corner for being naughty, that I'd asked for the keys before she had told me to. I stood in the corner and she was standing behind me flicking my ears and telling me I had been naughty and deserved to be punished. I felt like a small boy and was really seething inside but I couldn't do anything. In real life my wife is in control, and I guess I hate this."

BELOW LEFT Sometimes we may wonder who is pulling the strings. Our dreams can show us who is running the show and what we can do to take more charge of our lives.
BELOW It is easy for an adult to overpower a child when he wants to assert his authority. This can create a fear of authority, which we carry as adults.

WARS AND BATTLE

ABOVE Many societies recognize warrior values such as strength and courage. When a warrior appears in your dreams it may mean that you need to develop such qualities.
ABOVE RIGHT If images of war haunt our dreams we may feel very shocked or disturbed. But being in conflict is something that can happen in personal relationships or you may be fighting with yourself.

ALTHOUGH NOT MANY OF US WILL HAVE ACTIVELY PARTICIPATED IN ARMED COMBAT, THERE IS ALWAYS A WAR BEING FOUGHT IN SOME PART OF THE WORLD THAT WE ARE AWARE OF AND PERHAPS CONCERNED ABOUT. ACTS OF INTERNATIONAL TERRORISM UNSETTLE US AND MAKE US ANXIOUS FOR OUR SAFETY, OR PERHAPS WE LIVE IN A NEIGHBOURHOOD BESET BY GANG CONFLICT. OUR FEARS OF DEATH AND DESTRUCTION, INJURY, INVASION, INSECURITY, HELPLESSNESS, SORROW, PAIN AND LOSS RISE TO THE SURFACE, AND IN TIMES OF WAR OUR DREAMS CAN BECOME EVEN MORE VIVID.

THE ENEMY

Dreams of war don't necessarily reflect the belligerent or defensive attitude of a nation – they are quite likely to be more to do with acting out our own private battles. Our dreams reflect why we are under attack or what we are fighting for.

Identifying the enemy and understanding what they symbolize is crucial in analysing such a dream, as is the matter of which party is the aggressor. If the war represents a power struggle or a fight over scarce resources, it is also important to understand who has the upper hand. Are you retaliating for something that has already happened, or defending yourself against an ongoing attack? Perhaps you feel invaded by a particular person or circumstance in your life, and you have to defend your "territory", or someone is bullying or abusing you and you are too frightened to fight back in real life.

It may even be that you are simply recognizing the need to be more assertive, or that you are not being taken notice of and realize that spectacular action is required in order to get through.

ALLIES AND FIGHTING STRENGTH

We also need to ask questions about our own side – whether we are fighting alone or have allies, and if so how organized and how strong they are, and what kind of tactics they use. Our own attitude and that of the people around us is important. We may feel passionately that there is a lot at stake, and that this is a war worth waging, but equally the war could be something we are forced to participate in against our will; for a pacifist, it may be complete anathema. If others seem keen, but we are not, then this could indicate some disharmony with the people we do things with in a team of some kind. A formally organized army may well bring up feelings around authority and discipline,

DREAM OF WAR

"I was a soldier stalking an unseen enemy, a sort of sniper in a ruined city. I followed every move of the enemy, but knew that although I was the hunter I was going to get killed. Sure enough, as I turned a corner this faceless soldier let me have it. I was blown away.

For me this was about acting aggressively because this is expected of me as a man. As a sniper I may have seemed to have the advantage, but actually I was just hiding because I was afraid that I would eventually meet my match, and didn't know when or where that might happen, or who it might be."

leadership and obedience. Being armed could signify being ready for the fight – either feeling aggressive or being prepared.

If you are not evenly matched against your opponents, though, and using bows and arrows against an enemy with firepower, you will feel the disadvantage keenly. Depending on the exact nature of the dream, actually using arms may signify either being in control of a situation or having lost it.

THE SETTING

On land, on the sea or in the air, in a jungle or a desert, or even in the streets of a city – the terrain will suggest the underlying mood of the conflict. Particularly note whether you have a clear view, and if you know where you are going, as these can indicate some clarity on the issues over which you are at war.

PERSONAL BATTLES

War in a dream is often a metaphor for the personal battles and struggles of our everyday lives. If in your dream you are

being invaded, try to feel whether there is something or someone who is invading your space. If you are waging war in your dreams, then look at conflict situations in your waking life, and whether people you have a lot of contact with are being aggressive or overbearing.

BELOW War is also about its after-effects, and the devastation that follows in its wake.

If you are defeated or outmanoeuvred in your dream, see whether you are feeling defeated or manipulated over a real issue. Also note what you are feeling in the dream – fear, anger, sadness, confusion or rebellion may all play a part and relate to events in your life. If you can identify these situations and feelings you are more likely to be able to take appropriate action.

ABOVE In our dreams, the landscape in which the conflict takes place may give us a clue as to what the dream is about.
ABOVE LEFT There are many ways of symbolizing victory. What would it look like in your dreams?
ABOVE FAR LEFT The battle for resources is one of the reasons we humans go to war.

TROUBLE AHEAD

OUR DREAMS OFTEN DROP HINTS ABOUT HOW THE FUTURE MAY UNFOLD. ALTHOUGH THERE ARE OCCASIONS WHEN PEOPLE HAVE HAD DREAMS THAT SEEMED TO PREDICT SPECIFIC EVENTS, MORE USUALLY THE INFORMATION IN OUR DREAMS IS OUR UNCONSCIOUS MIND'S WAY OF TRYING TO ALERT OUR ATTENTION TO THINGS THAT MAY HAPPEN IF WE CARRY ON DOING WHAT WE'RE DOING, RATHER THAN PREDICTING THAT SOMETHING IS DEFINITELY GOING TO HAPPEN. SYMBOLS OF WARNINGS IN OUR DREAMS MAY BE AS SIMPLE AS THE WARNINGS WE RECEIVE IN DAILY LIFE. SUCH DREAMS CAN BE TRICKY TO INTERPRET AS IT MAY NOT BE CLEAR WHAT THE SYMBOLS RELATE TO.

WARNINGS

In general, the modern Western view is that our dreams exist primarily as a means of communication between our unconscious and conscious selves. Other cultures, however, have believed that our dreams can tell us of impending trouble and have used the information as a basis for their subsequent actions. There is plenty of anecdotal evidence to support this view. Famously, the American president Abraham Lincoln dreamed of his own death, which to the great interest of dream analysts ever since, he left an account of.

Unfortunately Lincoln did not heed the warning the dream contained, and met with an early demise. Still, we have no proof that it was not mere coincidence, or evidence of what must be a common fear among those with a high political profile. While dramatic dreams such as Lincoln's are the ones that seize our imagination, part of our fascination with predictive dreams lies in how we are able to foresee such an event, and what, if anything, we should do about it. If we were to alter our behaviour to protect ourselves from the possibility that every negative dreamt experience will come true, our lives would be blighted by paranoia and become an impossible nightmare.

READING THE CLUES

Our dream warnings may be less clear than a scenario of impending death, though. More typically, the warnings we receive in dreams will be of conditions or future events of which we are already aware but are trying to ignore, or that we could foresee if we took the trouble or the courage to notice the signs. Our lives are filled with stimuli, so it is not always possible to notice everything consciously, but these dreams allow us to become aware of the fact that we are not seeing or hearing something that we need to. In fact our unconscious may remind us of this by literally making us blind or deaf in our dreams, or by giving vivid or exaggerated pictures – either symbolic or literal – of our situation.

DANGER SIGNS

In real life, dangers are often helpfully signposted using fairly universal symbols. Traffic signs warn of hazards on the road, the

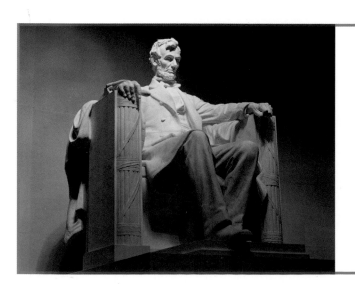

LINCOLN'S DREAM

It is easy with hindsight to interpret a dream as a precognition. These are the words of Abraham Lincoln as he recounted his dream in which he had foreseen his own death at the hand of an assassin.

"There seemed to be a death-like stillness about me. I heard subdued sobs, as if many people were weeping. I feel that I left my bed and walked downstairs. I went from room to room. No living person was in sight, but the same mournful sounds of distress met me as I passed along. I kept on until I arrived at the East Room, where I met with a sickening surprise. Before me was a catafalque, on which rested a corpse wrapped in funeral vestments. Around it were guards and a throng of mourners, many weeping pitifully. 'Who is dead in the White House?' I demanded of one of the soldiers. 'The President,' was his answer. 'He was killed by an assassin.'"

stylized image of the skull and crossbones is used to signify poison and other similar dangers, while "keep out" signs warn you that you are about to trespass on private property. If such symbols appear in your dreams, you can take them as an indication of some danger or difficulty you are headed for, given your present circumstances or actions.

An alarm fitted to your house or car may point to feelings of insecurity or vulnerability, either around your physical being or possessions, or around your sense of self. You may feel that you need to protect yourself from attack, or from losing things that are significant. If the alarm is ringing, there may be more of a sense of urgency in these feelings, as though you are already in danger, it is important to take such a clear warning seriously.

DECODING A SITUATION

Sometimes the benefit of heeding a warning lies in the process of working out what it is about. The next step is to actively take on board the significance and

implications of a situation, and in such cases our unconscious may present us with more obscure signs. If we can decode them, we will understand how to adjust our lives. For instance, you may dream of a realistic situation in your present life getting out of control. From this you may conclude that you need to make some adjustments about how you relate to the people in that situation; or that your life is going too fast and you must slow down; or that you need to take control of this aspect of your life.

RECURRING DREAMS

If you repeatedly dream of something that worries you, take whatever action you feel necessary to set your mind at rest. It doesn't mean that your dreams are foretelling things that will definitely go wrong, they are merely drawing your attention to a possible problem.

Recurring dreams can be an attempt by our unconscious to point out when we are ignoring danger; the dream may be repeated over and over again until we do something about it.

ABOVE Sometimes the mood or atmosphere in a dream can make us feel uneasy and could be a warning of trouble ahead.
ABOVE LEFT Warning dreams are not easy to interpret. It may not be clear whether the warning is of an event about to happen or is a metaphor for personal issues.

BELOW When life is not going our way it is easy to feel a victim. Perhaps your dream is about improving your own circumstances. Maybe you need to take more control and stop blaming the "hand of fate"?

DANGERS

EVERY NOW AND AGAIN OUR DREAMS SEEM TO COME TO US SPECIFICALLY TO TELL US OF DANGER, USING METAPHORS FOR WHATEVER DIFFICULTIES OUR UNCONSCIOUS BELIEVES WE MIGHT BE IN. WHEN PLANE CRASHES, NATURAL DISASTERS, OR ACCIDENTS IN THE HOME FIGURE IN OUR DREAM NARRATIVE THEY MAY SIGNAL SPECIFIC PROBLEMS IN OUR LIVES THAT COULD LEAD US INTO TROUBLED TIMES. THEY MAY BE TELLING YOU ABOUT SPECIFIC FEARS THAT HAVE ARISEN BECAUSE OF THE SUPPOSED DANGERS THEY MAY PRESENT, OR TIE IN TO EVENTS THAT HAVE ALREADY OCCURRED IN YOUR LIFE AND WHICH YOU ARE AFRAID MIGHT HAPPEN AGAIN. THEY MAY EVEN BE COMPLETELY IRRATIONAL.

DANGEROUS PEOPLE

Threatening behaviour by other people is a common sign of social or emotional trouble. We might dream of being attacked – an intruder with a knife, a crazed lunatic rushing at us out of nowhere, someone grabbing us from behind. The attack may represent a personal threat rather than a physical one, for example if you have a bullying or critical boss or a domineering partner. Such scenarios may well be warnings, indications that our unconscious actively believes we are under attack or being overwhelmed by someone, and it is best to take notice of what such dreams are telling us.

NATURAL DISASTERS

In some dreams we might be threatened by dramatic events of nature – lightning, avalanche, storm, flood, earthquake, meteor strike – and again we should take note of these dreams. They have a symbolic intent, to warn us that we may feel insecure, out of control and at the mercy of fate, or overwhelmed. Different types of disaster are likely to place emphasis on different aspects of our being – for instance flooding can relate to the emotions, fire to passion or anger, an avalanche or earthquake to the stability of our lives – although the details will vary from person to person. All are disruptive, but in their upheaval they may also suggest a purging of some central aspect of our lives, sweeping away all that has gone before so that we can start afresh.

DANGER IN THE HOME

The dangers of our dreams can be minor domestic mishaps like getting an electric shock from a faulty plug, losing or breaking something we value, or the kitchen being flooded due to a blocked drain. Such dreams could be warnings of real dangers

---

DREAM OF DANGER

"I was walking along a dark, rural lane. It had been raining and the trees were dripping black water. Suddenly I felt myself grabbed from behind and thrown to the ground. I remember, in my dream, worrying more about my coat getting wet than about what was to happen to me. I felt I knew the person who had attacked me, even though I couldn't see his face. He stood over me in a very threatening attitude with his fists clenched. This dream seemed so real that I didn't feel I could ignore it, and I spent ages trying to work out who my attacker was. I came to the conclusion that he represented a colleague I worked very closely with but had never really trusted. I had a quick look at his work later that day and found he had been taking my ideas and passing them off as his, and I had been literally 'in the dark' about his behaviour for some time."

that could actually occur in our waking lives. We may have seen but ignored the signs of an "accident waiting to happen" – a frayed wire, a blocked drain – and this is our unconscious mind's way of bringing these defects to our notice and making sure that more serious mishaps don't happen. But they may also be symbolic rather than literal – pointing to discord in the home or fears around a multitude of issues to do with loss or damage or danger.

A more calamitous event, such as the house falling down, could indicate difficulties around your security, stability or domestic situation, while a dream of being trapped in a house on fire may be a powerful metaphor for how you feel about some central aspect of your life.

EMOTIONAL OUTCOMES

The accident or disaster in your dream may be intended as a catalyst for some behaviour or emotion rather than a sign of danger. For instance, you may have feelings of guilt or blame around some completely different scenario in your life where things are not working out – maybe you need to express these feelings and work with them. Or you may be contemplating failure, especially of something that you see as being very important – perhaps your plans or dreams for the future are going awry and the life journey you had envisaged for yourself is being abruptly curtailed. But in every disaster a hero emerges, and it could be that you are seeking to take on this role – to gain recognition for strength or bravery, or love.

ABOVE Our unconscious is infinitely creative in the way it produces its dream images. Being in a precarious situation is highlighted by this image. It may indicate things slipping out of control.

LEFT In dreams, as in waking life, danger can come at us from any direction and from where we least expect it.

CHANGE AND IMPERMANENCE

WHEN THINGS ARE GOING WELL IT IS FAIRLY NATURAL TO WANT THEM TO LAST THAT WAY FOREVER. BUT CHANGE IS ACTUALLY ONE OF THE FEW CERTAINTIES WE HAVE IN LIFE AND OUR DREAMS OFTEN DROP HINTS ABOUT HOW THE FUTURE MAY UNFOLD. WHATEVER OUR SITUATION IS NOW, IT IS SURE TO BE DIFFERENT SOON. WE MIGHT BE ENERGIZED BY THIS PROSPECT AND FIND IT EXCITING, OR WE MAY FIND IT THREATENING AND SCARY. WE MAY EVEN REFUSE TO BELIEVE IT COULD BE TRUE. BUT NO MATTER WHAT OUR ATTITUDE, THERE IS NO GETTING AWAY FROM THE FACT THAT CHANGE IS A NATURAL AND INEVITABLE PART OF LIFE AND OUR SUBCONSCIOUS MIND WILL BE DEALING WITH IT IN OUR DREAMS.

CONSTANT CHANGE

There is a story of a king who asked his advisers to come up with a saying that would be true for all time, no matter what situation we find ourselves in. The advisers thought long and hard but were defeated, so the king turned to a Buddhist monk who said, "This too shall pass." This was the phrase the king had been looking for.

This story illustrates the point that change is inevitable. The changes we experience may be more or less noticeable at different points in our lives.

Some, such as having a baby, getting married or divorced, or leaving school, will be major and will alter the course of our lives and the roles we play. Other changes will be more subtle and may have more to do with our inner world – our feelings and perceptions change over time and affect the way we relate to others.

RESPONDING TO CHANGE

Some changes are self-generated, and we have some control over them. We are able to decide what happens and when. But often change is out of our control and can take us on a journey that we didn't intend. These sorts of changes, such as losing a partner or a job redundancy, may be scary as we have to adjust to an unknown that is not of our choosing. Changes that are forced on us can be useful and welcome or they can provide setbacks – whether we resist or "go with the flow" will make a huge difference as to how well we cope.

How we respond to change is reflected in our dreams. If we cope well, then change may be symbolized by something that is fluid or flowing, such as a running brook or clouds moving across an open sky. If the change is dramatic or important, then an image of transformation, like that of a caterpillar turning into a butterfly, or a chicken hatching from an egg, may appear. If we are finding it difficult to cope with change, then the symbolism may be more intimidating, such as dreaming that our teeth are falling out. Our unconscious will always provide the clues about what is happening.

TRANSITION

As we move through life, we leave behind the behaviours and attitudes of one phase to move into something new: when one door closes another opens. Such

BELOW Our dreams will reflect how we view change and how we adjust to the unknown. Do we hanker for the past, or are we able to move with the times? Consider what an image like this steam train could mean in your dreams.

times of transition are not always easy. We may find it hard to adjust to losing our youth for instance, or when we discover that our thoughts and feelings are outdated. Like a bird learning to fly, we have to find new ways of coping with life as we settle into each different phase.

At such times, our dreams may be filled with images of running away, travelling or exploring; in such activities we may be searching for the energy of more youthful pursuits; trying to escape from the narrowing of focus that often goes with the ageing process; or, in a more positive light, we may be discovering the value of our present lives and looking forward to some kind of transition.

TRANSFORMATION

Some dream images can be frustratingly fluid. In a second our surroundings may have transformed, through the shapes and colours of objects, the size or layout of a room, or a person's character. We are more flexible than we imagine, and often it is a

RIGHT Whether we find change easy or difficult will depend to some extent on our attitude. Our dreams may show us scenes from nature to remind us that every ending also contains the seeds of a new beginning.

matter of courage or imagination to see how wonderful change can be. On the other hand, we may use our dreams to confront or justify our fears of change and difference, or of uncertainty about the stability of a situation. Transformation in our dreams can guide us in how to make positive changes in our lives and overcome our resistance to things being different.

ABOVE All change is a metamorphosis of one sort or another – things changing from what they were to what they will become. Some of these changes will feel weird or unsettling in our dreams.
ABOVE LEFT Change lies hidden beneath the surface of what we can already see, and is something of a mystery.

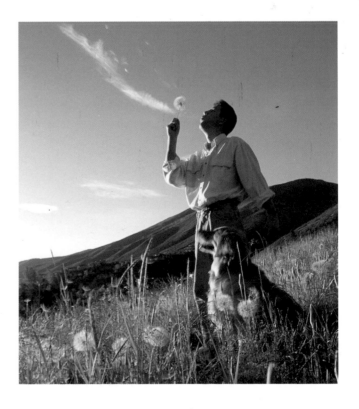

DREAM OF CHANGE

"I was chasing mice, trying to get them back into their cage, but each time I caught one it suddenly rotted in my hand. I was panicking and running everywhere trying to keep these mice in. I wanted to scream at them 'Stay in the cage or you'll go to pieces'.

My children were leaving home, and it was very unsettling; I didn't know what to do with myself and I felt left behind. Each mouse in the dream was a child. I wanted them to stay in the cage with me. If I have to stay why shouldn't they have to as well? I also worried about how they would cope in the big wide world and wanted to stop them from leaving, but I suppose in my heart I knew that this was a change they needed to make whatever I felt about it ."

MOVEMENT, MACHINES AND STRUCTURES

Our dreams are often signals of change and progress, and movement, machinery and structures can be connected with these things. We all use machinery of one kind or another. It enables us to effect changes, and mould our environment to our needs and taste. Technology means that both the machinery and the things we can do with it are constantly evolving. This evolution may be challenging and exciting, but for many it is stressful and bewildering. It is easy to feel lost as if in a maze of new ideas. Alternatively we seek security in the structures we create – the comfort and safety of our homes or other buildings. Sometimes we don't know whether we are coming or going and we may try to escape from it all by flying or running away, or going on a journey. Indeed movement, whether of ourselves or of things in our surroundings, can signify change and show us how at ease we are with ourselves and our environment.

FLYING AND FALLING

OUR DREAMS RELEASE US FROM THE CONSTRAINTS OF OUR EARTHBOUND LIVES, AND SO IT IS NOT UNCOMMON IN OUR UNCONSCIOUS FANTASIES TO FIND THAT WE CAN FLY. AS WELL AS A SENSE OF RELEASE AND FREEDOM, FLIGHT MAY GIVE US A DIFFERENT PERSPECTIVE ON OUR WORLD, THOUGH IN MANY DREAMS IT INVOLVES LITTLE MORE THAN SKIMMING OVER THE SURFACE OF THE GROUND. DREAMING OF FALLING IS LESS LIKELY TO BE A PLEASANT EXPERIENCE, BOTH IN THE PHYSICAL SENSATIONS IT MIGHT CAUSE, AND ALSO BECAUSE FALLING OFTEN POINTS TO THE PRESENCE OF TROUBLES AND A SENSE OF BEING OUT OF CONTROL THAT WE MIGHT BE CARRYING IN OUR WAKING LIVES.

CONFRONTING OUR INNER FEARS

For some people dreams of flying and falling may be an attempt to confront a fear of heights or to deal with vertigo – the dizziness we experience when our sense of balance has been disturbed. You can actually reprogramme your subconscious before you go to sleep with an instruction like "if I dream of flying or falling I will have wings and come to no harm". If you repeat this instruction to yourself often enough, then in your dreams you will indeed develop wings and cope better with the sensations in the dream.

There have been cases of people so terrified of having dreams of flying or falling that they resist the onset of sleep. For some, learning to sleep with a

BELOW RIGHT Flying in our dreams can be a positive experience and we can learn a lot from it. It can feel very liberating to find ourselves free from the constraints of the everyday world.
BELOW Dreams of flying or falling can be so scary and realistic that some people are too afraid to go to sleep in case they have such a dream.

pillow or cushion pressed up against the soles of their feet helps, as this stimulates the sensors in the feet and the sense of balance is restored, so there is no unconscious worry about being in freefall.

THEORETICAL INTERPRETATIONS

Freud and his followers maintain that for men dreams of flying are often associated with sex, while for women falling dreams may indicate succumbing to sexual temptation. Another school of thought says that flying and falling dreams point to the existence of a soul which can leave the body while we are asleep, and that such dreams are merely echoes or memories of these out-of-body experiences. Others still have said that falling

dreams indicate the presence of internalized fears around our ambitions – the fear of falling from power or position.

PERSONAL INTERPRETATIONS

Any of these interpretations may be true in some circumstances, but since our dreams are personal to us, we also need to take into account our situation, experience and feelings, together with the details of the dream itself, before we can try to understand what it means.

Flying in our dreams is often quite a positive and liberating experience, as it suggests that we have shed the physical limitations of being earthbound. Flying high can be aspirational – think of the concept of "soaring to new heights" – or it could suggest that we are seeking a new perspective on some aspect of our lives. We may find ourselves "flying in the face of something", trying to escape from the narrowness of social conventions or the dull routine of daily life perhaps, or it could be something more urgent or threatening that we are trying to escape from. Our dream flight could just be the frustrating business of not being able to get airborne, despite a monumental effort to do so, in which case you should look closely at what is holding you back; similarly see if there are any obstructions or other difficulties in flying, as these could indicate things that are hindering you in your life.

Falling may be liberating, but it is more likely to be linked to a loss or reduction of some kind, such as falling from power or from grace. It may represent loss of control – hence the expression "falling in love" – or it may be about getting into trouble. We talk of "falling out of favour" or even just "falling out" with someone, and any of these could be suggested in your dreams. The

RIGHT Dreams of falling may jolt us awake with a start as we come to "land". Notice what it is in your dream that breaks your fall – is it something soft and safe or is it more precarious? What does this mean to you?

feeling of falling into an abyss may point to the actual process of falling asleep, losing consciousness, or losing awareness or sensation. In any case, note whether you catch on to something while you fall, which could indicate a reprieve or point to something that might help you. Also see whether the landing – if it happens – is hard or soft, and what you land on – you may land in a safety net or plunge into a pool of water.

FLIGHTS OF FANCY

If you lie down and close your eyes, the resulting loss of visual stimulation means that you concentrate much more on your other senses. Physical sensations are particularly intense. But within a few minutes your body will probably be so relaxed that you will feel little other than your breathing. Concentrating on the

rhythm of your breathing in this way gives a sensation of movement. Add to this the lack of visual stimulation, the relaxed bodily posture, plus sleepiness, darkness and quiet, and you have pretty well all you need to imagine you are flying. The same goes for falling. If you lie down, close your eyes and roll your eyes upwards, the sensors in your feet that tell your brain about your spatial orientation and position get turned off, and your brain assumes that you are in freefall. The feelings of flying and falling that the brain generates may get translated into dream material.

BELOW LEFT The desire for flight has always been a source of fascination for us. Until we invented machines to help us fly, we could only experience it in our dreams.
BELOW It is not by chance that we use the phrase "falling asleep". The physical sensations are similar to falling, which may explain where some of our falling dreams come from.

PURSUIT

WE DO NOT ALWAYS KNOW WHAT WE ARE RUNNING FROM IN OUR DREAMS. OUR PURSUER MAY BE SOME UNKNOWN FORCE OR TERRIFYING POWER, AND IT IS IMPORTANT TO ESTABLISH WHAT IT SYMBOLIZES. IT IS OFTEN THOUGHT TO BE OUR FEARS IN SOME FORM OR ANOTHER, BUT IT MAY EQUALLY BE ASSOCIATED WITH CONFLICT. TO COME TO TERMS WITH THE CONFLICTS IN OUR LIVES WE NEED TO ACCEPT OR CONFRONT THEM RATHER THAN AVOID THEM, HOWEVER FRIGHTENING THEY MAY BE, AND PURSUIT DREAMS CAN HELP US TO DO THIS. BY ASKING OURSELVES THE QUESTION "WHAT AM I RUNNING AWAY FROM IN MY WAKING LIFE?" WE MAY FIND THE KEY TO WHAT OUR PURSUIT DREAMS ARE ALL ABOUT.

LEFT Are you being pursued or are you watching a chase unfold? Perhaps you are the pursuer? You might, of course, be all the elements of the chase, all this needs to be assessed as you try to interpret what this feeling of pursuit means to you.

representing our hidden inner conflicts. But in some dreams we may have the courage to turn around and confront our pursuer, to face issues that we need to face, to challenge and stand up to the people who are causing us misery. In these cases, the dreams may be about dealing with conflict in our lives.

Conflicts can come at us from all sorts of sources – work, love, sex, money, children and countless others – and often have no easy solution. How we handle the chase in our dreams will

BELOW Pursuit does not have to mean a physical chase. It is possible to feel we are under scrutiny, or pursued by threats or feelings. Look closely at your dream symbolism to discover what is happening to you.

RUNNING FROM FEAR

Often in our dreams we are running from people, things or situations that make us frightened or anxious. We may not know what it is we are running from, although we may

have strong feelings around it or a clear sense of its qualities. It could even be that we are running away from some aspect of ourselves that we dislike or feel uncomfortable with, and we can see this type of dream as show us something important about how we are handling the conflict we are trying to address.

If the pursuit dream is a recurring one we do have the ability to reprogramme ourselves so that we can, in our dream, stop and turn around and see what is pursuing us. We could also use techniques such as gestalt to work with the material. But if it is a one-off dream and we don't have that opportunity, then we should investigate the underlying fears or conflicts that it presents.

Feeling that your legs are tied, or that you are unable to move no matter how hard you try is quite common in pursuit dreams. This may be associated with the REM stage of sleep where we relax so deeply that we cannot move a muscle. When we go to sleep our brain shuts down our physical movements and we go into a kind of natural paralysis – perhaps to make sure that our dreams don't literally run away with us. But it can also symbolize

RIGHT We may feel threatened in a dream by vague fears or a shadowy figure but not have a clear sense of what it really is that is making us feel uneasy.
MIDDLE RIGHT The threat of pursuit may become more tangible as our fears grow monstrous.
BOTTOM RIGHT Another way of approaching pursuit dreams is to view the pursuer as an aspect of yourself that wants your attention.

feeling helpless, trapped or tied down to something when you want to be able to escape.

GIVING CHASE

There may of course be dreams in which we are the ones doing the chasing. To interpret these dreams we should look at who or what we are pursuing and what they mean to us. Then we need to examine our lives to see what dreams we chase, what ambitions remain unfulfilled, what goals we have yet to satisfy. The dreams we chase may be nebulous, dark, unspoken, unshaped, but once we turn the spotlight on them and think about what they may mean, they do in the end tend to become recognizable.

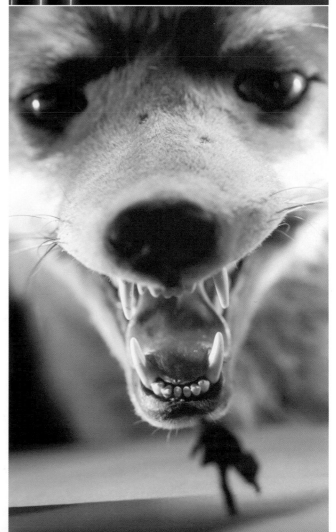

RUNNING FROM A PROBLEM

"I had this dream in which I was being chased by what seemed to be a patch of darkness. I felt there was something or someone within the darkness; I couldn't see it, but it seemed big and powerful and dangerous, and I felt that it could hurt me emotionally in some way. I was running but not getting anywhere because my feet were tied up with rope. The patch of darkness was almost upon me when I woke up.

When I was awake I went through my life to try and find out what my deepest concerns are. It wasn't difficult to work out. My husband has been offered an excellent opportunity in the city and wants us all to move, but I am happy where we are and feel the children's schooling is better here and that being settled and happy should take priority over his career move. This is causing me a lot of upset at the moment. In my dream I think the patch of darkness represented the forces of fate that were about to overwhelm me. The dream stimulated me into being less passive, though, I am not a victim to fate, and I have become more assertive since."

Mazes and Being Lost

ABOVE A maze is a kind of puzzle that is designed to get us lost and it can be fun to find ourselves going round in circles. See what being in a maze means for you.
ABOVE RIGHT Any dream about getting lost has been given to help us find a way out of a confusing situation in our waking life. It would be foolish to overlook the opportunity.

Being lost in our dreams may be as simple as feeling lost in our waking life. Certainly the symbolic value of mazes and labyrinths in our dreams is about being lost. We may be lost through physical disorientation, confusion or misunderstanding, loss or loneliness or through other difficulties. The theme of being lost could also point to a more complex issue, however, and it is best not to jump to quick and easy conclusions, but take some time to work out the details of the dream and what they might mean.

Mazes and labyrinths both consist of a network of pathways, but while a maze is designed to get you lost, a labyrinth has a definite goal at its heart. There may be a whole system of forked paths and dead ends but they are there to steer you towards the centre, to stop you retracing your steps and finding your way out.

A maze will often take you round in circles before spitting you out where you first began. It isn't designed to take you inward and indeed may deliberately keep you from the centre.

BEING LOST

When we dream of mazes and labyrinths, what is important is finding out why we are lost, what it is that we are turning away from. We all encounter difficulties and fears from time to time, but while some of us get on with trying to work them out, others feel unable to address them immediately and prefer to set them aside until they feel strong or clear-headed enough to do so. For the latter, this may manifest as dreams in which we are lost or misled, where we can't find our way out of a situation or to a place of safety. We struggle in the maze, held captive by our confusion. The reason we are being given the dream is not necessarily to spur us on — although that may be part of it — but rather to give us some insight into how to get out simply and easily. The dream is like a map written in code, and we can

---

DREAM OF BEING LOST

"I was underground, caving in a series of potholes with a friend. He had the map but it fell into a pool of deep water. We were lost and the light from our helmet torches began to fade. We were standing in a cave with many exits. We were concerned that there were underground lakes we would fall into so we felt we had to go up. Suddenly a bat flew out of nowhere and disappeared up one of the shafts. We knew which way we had to go: the bat had shown us the way.

Later on I realized that I was feeling bad about my job. I had wanted to study biology but had done accounts because it seemed a more practical career choice. I guess the bat was telling me to start again, to be true to myself. Once I did this the whole of my life seemed to improve."

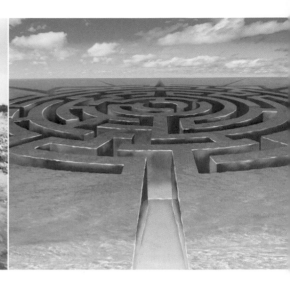

study our dream to see if we were helped through the dream maze by something or someone. This may be someone we know or a stranger; it may be some sort of angelic being or even an animal, wild or domestic.

THE CONFUSION OF CHOICE

Mazes and labyrinths often involve making a series of choices. If we make the right decisions we get to where we want to be, achieving a goal or clarity. If we make the wrong choices we remain lost, or land up where we began. It can be hard to remain clear-headed in such a situation, and if we are confused, making choices becomes a difficult process, and one in which we may easily make mistakes. The dream may well be helping us to make the choice based on intuition or on information that hasn't been accessible to our conscious mind.

The fact that we are in a maze in our dreams may even simply be warning us that some aspect of our lives is more complicated

than we thought, and that we should pay attention to the complexity of the choices we have to make. In your dream, look at the nature of your decision-making process – whether it is impulsive or random, or calm and rational, based on carefully weighed up factors. Notice whether it is

effective, and whether you are alone in the maze, and if not, does your companion help you or distract or mislead you? The answer to these questions may reveal the extent to which you can rely on others in your decision-making, how much trust you feel, or whether you want and are able to "go it alone".

ABOVE The symbolism of the stylized maze is a very powerful one, and one that your dream self will love to explore.
ABOVE LEFT Notice your surroundings in your dream. Are you where you want to be?
ABOVE FAR LEFT When we get our wires crossed, things get confusing. Our dreams may show us how to untangle the obstacles.

LEFT Are you lost and alone in your dream or is there someone who can lend you a helping hand? See if you can relate this to your life. Do you tend to struggle on alone because you find it hard to ask for support?

EXITS AND ENTRANCES

PHYSICALLY, AN ENTRANCE AND AN EXIT ARE SIMPLY TWO SIDES OF THE SAME OPENING, WHETHER IT IS A DOORWAY OR SOME OTHER KIND OF OPENING. ALTHOUGH THEY ARE PHYSICALLY IDENTICAL, WHAT DIFFERENTIATES ONE FROM THE OTHER IS YOUR VIEWPOINT AND WHICH WAY YOU PASS THROUGH. DOORWAYS MIGHT ALSO SYMBOLIZE A WHOLE VARIETY OF DIFFERENT THINGS IN YOUR LIFE; AN ENTRANCE OR AN EXIT MIGHT REPRESENT AN ESCAPE FROM A PROBLEM OR AN UNPLEASANT CIRCUMSTANCE, OR IT MIGHT BE A TEMPTATION TO ESCAPE FROM RESPONSIBILITY AND REALITY. WHEN YOU DREAM OF PORTALS YOUR INTERPRETATION WILL DEPEND ON THE CIRCUMSTANCES AROUND YOU.

BELOW Every exit is also an entrance and vice versa – it depends on which way we look at it.
BELOW RIGHT Dreams about exits and entrances may be trying to tell us something about the transitions that are going on in our waking life.

Freud would no doubt have attributed some sexual meaning to exits and entrances, while others suggest, for instance, that doors opening outward indicate a need to express yourself more and those opening inward a need to explore some aspect of your inner being. Each of these interpretations may fit in some circumstances, depending on the context in which the door appears in the dream and on your own circumstances. But even if they do fit, it is also important to find out more about the dream and how and why the doorway features – the kind of

entrance, whether it is you or someone else who is opening the door, and whether you are going in or out, for instance. It may be a small doorway, a huge gateway, or a cleft in a mountainside, and you should take note of the kind of structure it is part of as this may also be significant.

TRANSITIONS

An entrance or exit marks a transition from one space to another – spaces that may be similar, such as two rooms in a house, or quite different from each other, like an interior space and a garden. This could suggest

being at some kind of threshold or making an adjustment in your life, so look at how the transition works in your dream. Perhaps you make a grand entrance to the applause of a crowd, or you have to squeeze through, or maybe you slip between one dream scene and another without really noticing how you do so. These scenarios may all say something about how comfortable you are with the transition, whether or not you look forward to it, and how easy or difficult it is.

Every time you move from one space to another you are making an entrance and an exit at the same time, so it is worth looking at which aspect of the movement draws your attention – leaving or arriving, getting out of a place or going in. Sometimes you may be poised on the threshold itself, in a sort of limbo. How you feel about the space you are leaving behind as well as the one you are entering may also give important clues about the meaning of the transition – say, whether you have any regrets, or are relieved to be moving on. Whether or not you can retrace your steps will have a bearing on how easy it is to make your entrance or exit.

Transitions in your life may be physical ones, such as moving house, starting a new job, or going to live in a new country. But the entrances and exits in your dream can also be about emotional or spiritual thresholds, such as starting a brand new relationship or ending an existing one, or about the transition between consciousness and unconsciousness, or many others.

CLOSURE

Exits can be about achieving closure, about ending a period in your life or a way of being so that you can move on. You may need to start something afresh or begin a new venture, and it may be important for you to be able to leave behind any "baggage" you may have been carrying.

EXCLUSION

Sometimes the entrance in your dream is tantalizingly or frustratingly impassable; perhaps it's something that is perfectly visible but just beyond your reach. It may be a locked door, or a skylight up in the roof, or a barred window; if you encounter one of these, ask yourself if there are situations in your life from which you feel barred or excluded. Or perhaps you can see a way forward to something you want but are not sure how to get to it because there are obstacles in the way; if this is the case, see whether there was any

alternative route to the place you were trying to get to in your dream, or someone who could help you unlock the door or reach the skylight. These could suggest alternative ways of achieving what you are after in your waking life.

ABOVE Our dreams can show us that we have an opportunity to step out into new terrain.
ABOVE LEFT Sometimes the exits and entrances in our dreams are out of reach. We may want to go there, but it is impossible or too dangerous just now.

EXITS AND ENTRANCES DREAM

"There was a cocktail party going on in a large room that was accessed by a large door off a long corridor. There were lots of people standing around talking, smoking, eating and drinking. I kept walking in and out of this big doorway, I was the only one that was coming and going. Each time I came in I fell over, more and more drunk, and people kept turning round to look at me, but I didn't care. As soon as I went out and was standing in the corridor I was quite sober again.

For me, a cocktail party is the kind of boring, formal, old-fashioned function that older people like my parents would go to. The people at the party were all drinking, but they could handle it while I just got really drunk. But I was deliberately playing the fool each time I came in, perhaps as a way of rebelling against the older people.

I think the dream was actually about the prospect of joining my parents' business. I thought I'd come round to the idea but the dream showed that I haven't really – I actually find the business boring, and I think I'm too young to be getting into something like that! I'd rather find my own way through life, and do the kind of things my friends are doing."

BUILDINGS

LIKE US, BUILDINGS HAVE A LIFESPAN – THEY DEGENERATE, DECAY AND FALL INTO DISUSE. IN OUR DREAMS THEY COULD REPRESENT US AND WE MAY NEED TO LOOK AT WHAT POINT IN OUR OWN LIFE THE BUILDING IS TRYING TO BE. SOME DREAM INTERPRETATIONS SUGGEST THAT BUILDINGS REPRESENT THE DREAMER'S BODY, AND THIS DOES SEEM TO FIT WITH SUCH EXPRESSIONS AS "MY BODY IS A TEMPLE". BUT IF THE STRUCTURE IN YOUR DREAM ISN'T A TEMPLE BUT AN ART DECO CINEMA SHOWING OLD GANGSTER MOVIES, OR A DISUSED TIN MINE, OR HIGH-RISE CITY OFFICE BLOCKS, YOU MAY NEED TO EXPLORE MORE DEEPLY WHAT THE STRUCTURE MEANS TO YOU. IT IS ALSO POSSIBLE THAT ONLY PART OF A BUILDING IS RELEVANT.

In some cases you can take the buildings in your dreams at face value – as nothing more than a literal part of the scenery. Your unconscious has to set the dream somewhere and a building you know well may be used because it is a familiar and appropriate setting for the events of the dream. If the surroundings fit then you can probably discount them, but if the building is strange or unusual or disjointed in any way though, you need to look closer.

TYPES OF BUILDING

The function of the building in your dream could be a big clue to its meaning. For example, churches or temples are likely to be associated with your spiritual side or your relationship to religion, while a bridge may signify that you need to cross some obstacle or forge a link between two people or things or ideas. Underground structures, such as basements, mines or cellars, may be particularly relevant if you are currently in the process of exploring and uncovering deeply rooted personal issues. And you are likely to have quite different feelings around an industrial building such as a factory or power plant from those connected with a little cottage.

Different people will also have different responses to the same setting – for instance, you may find a factory a noisy, smelly and confusing or overwhelming place to be, but for someone else its salient feature could be that it is to do with mass-production or innovation and newness, in which case it could be to do with innovation or progress in some important aspect of their life.

APPEARANCE

Particular qualities of the building may come to your attention and have specific relevance – either the materials or the style, the state of repair, or perhaps some element such as a chimney or staircase.

The clean lines and cold, reflective materials of a modern building may suggest orderliness or control in your life, forward-thinking or a detachment from your heritage, while a rustic cottage with rough wooden beams and a lived-in feel could indicate a feeling of comfort or security. Since our response to styles and materials is highly personal, however, you will need to see the building in the context of your own personal feelings and tastes.

The state of the buildings or other structures can provide another layer of significance to the basic meaning of the building. Clean and orderly or dirty, well maintained or falling apart – if you see the building as some aspect of your own being then the state of repair and cleanliness could indicate how you view yourself. A shabby or neglected building may be hinting that you need to look after yourself more, that you don't value yourself enough or suffer from low self-esteem.

BELOW There are probably as many different kinds of building as there are people. How you feel about them and what they represent in your dreams will be a matter of personal taste and association.

> The dream is an involuntary kind of poetry.
> JEAN PAUL RICHTER

ABOVE Some buildings will take on an otherworldly quality in our dreams, as though they are trying to tell us something very deep and instinctive.

ABOVE A staircase is how we go up or down and traditionally has been linked to a man's sexual prowess. What would you make of such an image in your dreams?

STAIRCASES

It is often said that a staircase is symbolic of a man's sexual prowess, ambition or career progress. It could mean any or none of these things, but notice how important it is in your dream – as in life, it could just have a practical function and simply be a means of getting about between floors in your dream narrative. If your unconscious wants to draw your attention to your sexual prowess, it may well choose a more obvious symbol.

In any case, it is worth considering that staircases allow you access to higher places, and that you may be using the stairs as a symbol for your ability to progress or achieve greater status; conversely descending a staircase may show a loss of these things. A staircase may also transport you between different states of consciousness or the higher and lower aspects of your being. Elevators and escalators may act in the same way as staircases, and help you on your way, but bear in mind that you are taking an "easy ride" by using them.

ABOVE A tall, upright building may represent a desire to be seen. Notice how the buildings appear in your dreams – are they new or old, clean or dirty?

ABOVE Buildings get old and fall into disuse. What would a dream of a ruined building mean for you? Is there something you have been neglecting and would like to repair?

RIGHT Factory buildings can appear alien and overpowering, although they may also represent work and progress.

BELOW How we view buildings in our dreams can tell us a lot about how we see ourselves. Here a city landscape towers above an area of domestic housing.

HOMES AND DWELLINGS

OUR HOUSES AND HOMES ARE EXTREMELY IMPORTANT TO US. EVEN BEFORE WE MOVE INTO A NEW PLACE, WE OFTEN MAKE ELABORATE PLANS ABOUT HOW TO MAKE IT OURS. WE DECORATE, RE-ORGANIZE THE ROOMS AND BUILD EXTENSIONS IN AN ATTEMPT TO PUT OUR PERSONAL STAMP ON IT. OUR AIM IS TO HAVE A HOME THAT IS SAFE, WARM, AND COMFORTABLE. IN OUR DREAMS A HOUSE IS OFTEN A MARK OF THESE THINGS AND CAN SHOW US ABOUT OUR SENSE OF SELF AND HOW SECURE WE FEEL. IF A HOUSE OR OUR HOME BECOMES A SCARY, THREATENING PLACE IN OUR DREAMS, THEN THAT MAY BE HOW WE VIEW IT IN OUR WAKING LIFE AND IT COULD BE SOMETHING WE NEED TO LOOK AT MORE CLOSELY.

A SAFE HAVEN

When we are at home we feel secure and more able to cope with the difficulties in our lives and the things that we find threatening. In our lives and our dreams alike, it can be a base to return to from our forays into a potentially dangerous and unpredictable world, and for many of us, the home is the centre of our life, our heart. The houses in our dreams are often familiar to us, and an obvious line of questioning you should pursue concerns the person who lives there, what they are like and what your relationship to them is. The home you grew up in or the house of a favourite aunt or grandparent is likely to be filled with a great many memories and reminders of your childhood, and could signify a nostalgia for these times, or perhaps be bringing to your attention an issue that arose at the time you were living there or visiting often.

ATTRIBUTES

If you dream of an unfamiliar house, it is the qualities of the building that are important. It is more likely to represent some aspect of yourself – your body, your personality, or your sense of who you are. You should ask yourself what it is about this particular building that has made you represent yourself in this way.

A big, grand house may show a need to expand your horizons or capabilities, to establish yourself more solidly, or to make a bolder statement to the world about yourself; on the other hand if you find in your dream, for instance, that you live in a mansion but are stressed by the upkeep, it may indicate that you feel you have taken on something that is bigger than you can handle. Equally, a small cottage may be cosy and comfortable or cramped and mean. If the house or furnishings are shabby, ask yourself if there is something you have done that would generate such a feeling. A tidy and well-maintained house may show a healthy self-regard or clarity of mind.

ROOMS

The rooms in a house allow us to compartmentalize aspects of our lives. Different areas of our lives may be represented by the function of particular rooms – the bedroom for sleep, sex and relaxation, the dining room for nourishment, the living room for leisure and sociability. So how you feel and what you are doing in each of these rooms could be

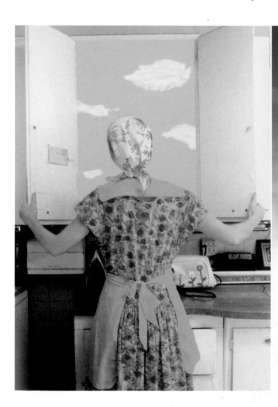

BELOW Our dreams often have a fairytale quality to them and can surprise us. Opening the kitchen cupboard to find fluffy white clouds inside could suggest a desire to be transported from the humdrum routine of domestic life.

HOMES AND DWELLINGS

RIGHT Colour and style create an impact. Do you feel at ease in your dream house or are you an uninvited guest?

BELOW LEFT Most of us aspire to owning our own home. Your dreams can show you how realistic your expectations are. **MIDDLE LEFT** We all have a stylized, idyllic image of perfect living. We may visit this place in our dreams for reassurance. **BOTTOM LEFT** To dream of a stately home or a large house may mean that we need to expand our horizons and "think big".

key to understanding how comfortable you are with these different aspects of your life.

Rooms are also said to represent your potential. If a room is familiar it signals your current or past capabilities, whereas an unfamiliar room could be showing you your unfulfilled potential; whether you are eager to explore it or back out and close the door may show how ready you are to realize that potential. Sometimes the houses in our dreams have hidden rooms or rooms that we are forbidden to enter. These may represent unexplored parts of ourselves or parts that we feel are taboo.

BUILDING A HOUSE

To dream of building a house might mean that you are interested in building greater security or turning an increase in prosperity into something concrete, though you will have to decide for yourself whether this type of interpretation seems correct. Different aspects of the building process may carry particular meanings as well. For instance, laying foundations may indicate establishing yourself, or creating a stable base for some project or aspect of your life.

Dreaming about a building project going awry could be about unforeseen problems or obstacles. Notice what building materials are being used and see what this means for you.

DREAM OF A ROOM

"My mother was driving me mad. I fled upstairs, but although there are only two flights of stairs in my house in real life, I ran up three flights of stairs in my dream. At the top I found myself in a lovely attic room, full of warmth and light and nice comfy chairs. It was decorated in wonderful lush fabrics and rich colours, and there was a smell of incense in the air. This seemed to be the happiest room I had ever been in and I felt so safe and comfortable here.

This was my own space, which I created in my dream as a refuge, a place where my troubles – in the form of my mother – could not follow me, and it was a place where I felt I could really be myself."

TOOLS AND MACHINES

THE DEVELOPMENT OF TOOLS AND MACHINES IS PART OF WHAT IT MEANS TO BE HUMAN. FROM THE EARLIEST TIMES, WE HAVE DEVELOPED TOOLS TO HELP US WORK MORE EFFECTIVELY AND TO INCREASE THE RANGE OF TASKS WE ARE CAPABLE OF PERFORMING. TOOLS AND MACHINES ENABLE US TO DO A MULTITUDE OF THINGS. THEY RANGE IN SIZE AND COMPLEXITY FROM THE SIMPLE PAPERCLIP TO THE VAST AND COMPLICATED STRUCTURE OF AN OIL-RIG OR SPACESHIP. OUR QUEST FOR PROGRESS AND IMPROVEMENT MEANS THAT TECHNOLOGY, WHICH BRINGS ABOUT THE CHANGES TO OUR TOOLS, OUR MACHINES AND MANY ASPECTS OF OUR ENVIRONMENT, IS AN EVER-PRESENT PART OF OUR LIVES.

TOOLS

When we think of tools the first thing that springs to mind may be carpentry or gardening equipment, but in fact we use all sorts of objects and even employ abstract ideas to manipulate our environment or to help us do a task – so a stick becomes a tool when we use it to draw in the sand or prop open a gate, and we can use our dreams as tools for understanding those issues in our lives to which we need to pay more attention.

In your dreams look for tools being used inappropriately or ones that are malformed or malfunctioning. If the person using the tool is right and the tool fits the purpose, then you could look beyond it to the job of work that is being done. Bear in mind though, that "rightness of fit" may in fact be just what your unconscious mind is trying to demonstrate: you need to use the right tool for the job.

MACHINES

There are also complex tools that enable us to undertake bigger and more complicated tasks. Machines do not require the same effort from us as hand tools as they have their own source of energy. This gives them a more human quality – they need fuel to work just as we need food; they emit waste; and some also look vaguely human. Sometimes we even give them names and refer to them fondly as "she" or "he". Because of this affinity to machines and the fact that we use them constantly, they may appear in our dreams as symbols for our own efforts and abilities.

BELOW MIDDLE Simple tools can symbolize complex issues: what do you need to sweep away?
BELOW RIGHT Being able to assemble things in a logical way is a skill that you may need to develop.
BELOW Computers are an integral part of modern life and can appear in our dreams in unusual ways.

MACHINE DREAM

"I was inside some sort of giant machine with cogs and wheels made of brightly coloured plastic, and a lot of wires and sparking electrical connections. I couldn't work out what this machine did, or what part of it I was in. I helped make it run but I had no idea how.

I had recently become a father, and the dream confirmed for me that however wonderful our baby was, I was extremely worried about my new role, about how to cope with the baby and how to understand his needs. The clue that linked the dream to my life situation was the plastic parts which reminded me of the Lego I played with as a child."

TECHNOLOGY DREAM

"I dreamt that I was trying to get my cash card into an ATM, but the card kept bending and slipping away; the more I pushed the softer it became and the less I could insert it. I suppose if I had been a man this dream would easily have been interpreted as being about impotence, but in my case I was anxious about some exams that were looming. I was worried that when I got into the exam room my brain would go soft and everything I had studied so hard to remember would slip out of my mind at the time when I most needed it. "

MACHINES IN DREAMS

Not all machines have a human quality. Sometimes they are big and impersonal, even menacing. Machines can be immensely powerful and unyielding – they can crush us if we get in the way, they tower over us and we can feel intimidated. They may even chase us, or simply have a dark and brooding presence. These qualities may mean the machines in our dreams become symbols of intimidation, of powerful forces or inevitability in the face of our powerlessness. Not knowing how to use a machine may also make us feel disadvantaged and we may employ this scenario in a dream to represent our frustrations or limitations.

FUNCTIONS

Often it is the function of the tool or machine that is important in our dreams. A dredger, for example, easily symbolizes the process of drawing up and bringing to light the contents of the murky depths. We might just have chosen a simple bucket and spade to dig up mud, but a full-size dredger is a more captivating and obvious image. In looking at the function of the tool or machine, also consider what it is the machine is acting on – what it is uncovering or burying, neatening off, transporting, shattering or moulding. Each of these actions may relate to something that is happening to you in your waking life.

TECHNOLOGY

In our dreams, technology may represent a threat to traditional values and ways of doing things, and may bring up feelings of fear or anxiety. For technology is a powerful symbol of movement and unstoppable change. This may leave us feeling left behind, confused or alienated, and it could also be a symbol for us to slow down. Technology can also represent cool efficiency and be tremendously empowering and exciting. It makes our lives easier and enables us to do a wider range of things more quickly and with less effort. Computers, mobile phones and DVD players as well as washing machines, cars and countless other devices are all part of modern technology and can appear in our dreams.

ABOVE Large machinery can symbolize a menacing and inhuman presence in our dreams. Check to see who or what is intimidating you and revisit the dream to see if it offers a clue about how to deal with the problem.

BELOW New technology allows us to bring the past into the present. Is there anything you need to update in your life? **BELOW LEFT** A tool that doesn't work properly hinders progress. Use your dream to check what isn't working in your life.

TRAVEL

IN DIFFICULT TIMES WE OFTEN WISH WE COULD ESCAPE, GET RIGHT AWAY AND LEAVE OUR TROUBLES BEHIND US RATHER THAN STRUGGLE ON WITH TRYING TO SOLVE THEM. WE MAY DREAM OF TRAVEL, OF BEING ON THE ROAD OR FLYING OFF INTO THE BLUE YONDER. BUT TRAVEL DREAMS ARE NOT ALWAYS ESCAPIST; THEY MAY REPRESENT OUR JOURNEY THROUGH LIFE AND THE PATHS WE TAKE, OR PERHAPS THEY REFLECT AN EAGERNESS TO BROADEN OUR HORIZONS. THEY ARE ALSO IMPORTANT SYMBOLS OF TRANSITION AND CHANGE — OUR DESIRE FOR SOME KIND OF CHANGE IN OURSELVES OR OUR CIRCUMSTANCES, OUR FEARS AROUND CHANGE, OR OUR NEED TO CHANGE.

ABOVE Travel dreams can show us where we are going in life. Notice if you are alone or with others, moving or stationary?
ABOVE RIGHT Seen from above, a complex network of roads may not look so confusing. Maybe a fresh perspective is called for?

THE JOURNEY

Because dream travels can be so varied, you will need to ask a number of questions about the nature of the journey in your dream – where you were going, the purpose of the journey, whether you were on foot or in a vehicle, travelling at speed or dawdling along. What the journey and the terrain were like and who your travelling companions were, if any, are also worth considering.

MAPS

If there was a plan or route involved in your travelling dream it is worth examining what they were like and what help they gave you. Maps can give you an overview of your journey and help you to plan a route or see where you are, but if they are unclear or misleading, don't

relate to the places you pass through, or you simply can't decipher them, this may suggest you are lacking direction in life.

DEPARTURES AND DESTINATIONS

Many a dream journey has no real starting point or end point. Instead you may simply have a

sense of being on the road to nowhere or needing to be on the move, or you may be exploring a place and seeing what it has to offer. These types of journey may have very different meanings. Not knowing where you are going can be highly significant, as it could show that you need to explore what you want out of

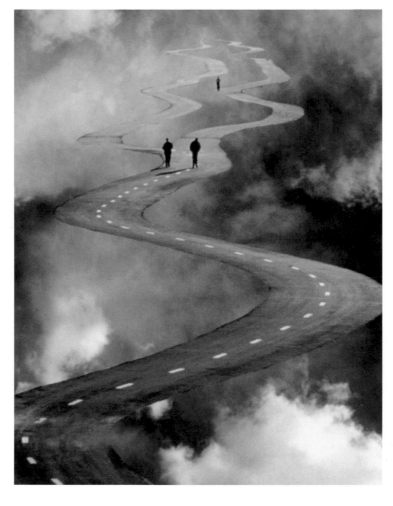

RIGHT Paths wind and diverge as we tread our way through life, and a dream may reflect this.

life, where you want your life journey to lead. On the other hand, it may be that getting left behind or being late may be the key issues, rather than where you are coming from or going to. If you do remember the beginning of your dream journey, it is worth looking at the starting point closely. It may represent something you are trying to run away from, or it could be a part of your past that you are ready to leave behind. The kind of departure may give a clue to which meaning is true for you.

Destinations are likely to be about goals and desires if you have chosen them, although they could equally be about situations that you are afraid of getting into if you don't seem to have control over where you are going.

TRAVELLING COMPANIONS

For the solo traveller, the journey may be a lonely one, but one in which you can be in charge, make all the decisions and take responsibility for whatever happens along the way. If you do have travel companions, though, ask yourself what they are like, whether they are people you know or not, and how they behave on the journey. A loving, supportive companion may indicate that there is someone you can take with you on your journey through life, while a person who hijacks your plans, dogs your footsteps, or insists on leading the way or having the best seat may be pointing to issues around people who are in some way interfering with your own plans.

People you meet along the way may help or hinder your journey, rescuing you from difficult situations or misleading you. These may be archetypal figures or may relate to actual people in your life who may be helping or obstructing your plans or goals.

LEFT Maps help us pinpoint where we are going. Is your map easy or hard to decipher?
MIDDLE LEFT Notice if your fellow travellers are good to be with or if they are annoying you.
FAR LEFT If your life feels like a long desert trek, remember that deserts also have their beauty and you can adapt to survive.

TRAVEL DREAM

"I had a dream in which travel was very prominent and obviously meant something important but I didn't know immediately what it was. I was crossing the Nevada desert in a red sports car, heading towards Las Vegas, where I was going to go gambling. Although I was alone, I could feel the presence of a blonde woman who may have just got out of the car.

I don't normally gamble in my waking life, but in relationships I can sail pretty close to the wind. I recently had a relationship with someone I was very fond of, and I now really regret messing her about. She was right to dump me. I guess I was gambling with her life and her future, and I lost. Maybe she was the woman who had just got out of my car in my dream. I think it's quite revealing that it was a red sports car as well. Although I don't own one it does symbolize the freedom and energy of youth to me."

MAGIC AND FANTASY

Magical, mystical people, mythical beasts, heroes and demons parade through our dreams, inspired by the fictions and superstitions of our culture and brought to life by our imagination as metaphors for our hopes and desires, for the irrational terrors of our early years, and even for the tricksters and con artists we meet as we go about our daily lives. We also use them to access possibilities beyond the mundane reality of everyday life, to help us shed the conventional boundaries that keep our imagination earthbound, and give us the courage to bring the seemingly impossible within our reach.

These dreams can be tremendously challenging as we can take nothing for granted in this fantasy reality, removed from the context of the here and now, and in them we confront our fears and demons head-on. The underlying universal truths of the archetypal figures we sometimes meet allow us to get in touch with our deeper, instinctive levels of being.

FANTASTICAL DREAMS

DREAMS IN WHICH LANDSCAPES, CHARACTERS, MOTIFS AND PLOTS ARE FANTASTICAL OR SURREAL ARE AMONG THE MOST DIFFICULT TO INTERPRET AS THEY ARE NOT BASED IN OUR EVERYDAY EXPERIENCES AND WE HAVE NONE OF THE USUAL REFERENCE POINTS TO HELP US. FANTASY DREAMS CAN BE VERY UNSETTLING, SHAKING US OUT OF ROUTINE OR COMPLACENCY. THEY RETURN TO HAUNT OUR WAKING THOUGHTS AND DEMAND THAT WE STRIVE TO UNDERSTAND THEM — SWEEPING THEM UNDER THE CARPET OR IGNORING THEM SIMPLY DOESN'T WORK. THEY MAY LINGER FOR A LONG TIME AND BE QUITE HARD TO PURGE FROM OUR CONSCIOUSNESS.

FANTASY CHARACTERS

Dreams sometimes feature fantastical creatures – gentle, dreamy unicorns and ferocious dragons, seductive mermaids, fairies and elves, talking animals and a myriad others we may have created with or without the assistance of literature or legend. The creatures of our fantasies are part of our desire for things to be beyond the real world.

These creations may return us to our childhood where monsters lurked under the bed and the line between reality and fantasy was much more indistinct. They may be frightening or disturbing, forcing us to address our fears head-on, but sometimes they are wonderful, joyful creatures that show us new possibilities or have unimaginable love or wisdom. They may have exceptional

powers, or take us to places that we can literally only dream of.

Creatures that we fabricate in our own minds, that are not found in myths or in the books we read as children, may have features that we take from several sources and combine into one character as a kind of catch-all for how we want to be or what we are most afraid of. It may be some idealized figure who will empower us, or a demon who threatens to destroy us.

FANTASY WORLDS

Dreams of fantasy may consist of unusual events or creatures set in surroundings that seem natural or familiar, or they may take place in weird and wonderful settings – a vast cavern that stretches upward as far as the eye can see, or the strange landscape

of another planet; we may be floating in nothingness or surrounded by permeable membranes that melt away, leaving us in a new setting. In fantastical environments even the laws of nature may be different – gravity may be stronger or weaker, we may be able to do things we can't normally do, such as flying – and social structures may be incomprehensible. Great battles or forces of good and evil confronting each other directly strip away the mundane detail of our real lives, along with the rules of politics and diplomacy.

The fictitious worlds of literature are as varied as they are fantastical. Some, such as Tolkien's Middle Earth or C.S. Lewis's Narnia, may look like places we could visit, but the creatures that inhabit them and

BELOW Our dreams are very close to the hidden, magical world of the unconscious and many dreams have a fairy-tale quality about them.
BELOW RIGHT In fantasy dreams, unusual or mythical creatures are the products of a rich and fertile imagination.

key elements of the plot could only be found in fantasy. Alice in Wonderland has an explicitly surreal dream setting, although it has realistic elements alongside its talking animals, mutations, and spatial distortions. Or the infamous world of Harry Potter shows us ordinary boys and girls who are able to slip out of family life into a world where they have magical powers: people walk through walls and play games in mid-air; cars can fly and animals have special powers. Perhaps part of the reason that all these stories are so popular is that they each explore archetypal themes, such as the use of power or the struggle between good and evil.

TRANSFORMATION

Like the hybrid animals of mythology, fantastical elements may involve the coming together of objects or beings that are normally quite distinct, or the transformation of one thing into

another. Material objects may take on unusual properties or space and time may be distorted. These transformations and mutations draw your attention to both the normal and the unusual properties of the objects or creatures, and you should try to reconcile both and notice what it is that is being distorted.

Fantasy dreams may represent all that we find exceptional about the world. They are our

unconscious mind's way of being inventive and unconventional and can help us work through some very human issues. Fantastical or magical dreams also remind us that we are much more than logic and reasoning. We are creatures with a powerful imagination and have the ability to devise creative solutions to our problems and answers to some of the big questions about our very existence.

ABOVE Art and literature can provide a stimulus for the unconscious in its nightly dream production. Check the landscape of your dreams to see if there is anything you recognize. Is the narrative running as it should or has the story changed?

I suspect that there are more things in heaven and earth than are dreamed of, or can be dreamed of, in any philosophy.

J. B. S. HALDANE

LEFT Children are usually fascinated by magic and fantasy, perhaps because they are much closer to their instinctive feelings than most adults.
FAR LEFT The fantasy images we produce in our dreams will have a cultural emphasis. Traditionally, fairies are magical creatures who use their powers to either help or hinder us.

MYTHS AND LEGENDS

OUR DISTANT ANCESTORS TRIED TO FIND EXPLANATIONS FOR THE MANY PHENOMENA OF NATURE IN THE WORLD AROUND THEM — THE SUN RISING, THE CHANGING SEASONS, AND CYCLES OF LIFE AND DEATH. BECAUSE THEIR KNOWLEDGE WAS LIMITED, THEY DEVISED EXPLANATIONS BASED ON THE EXISTENCE OF SUPERHUMAN BEINGS, GODS AND GODDESSES WHO NOT ONLY OFFERED AN EXPLANATION FOR WHY THINGS WERE THE WAY THEY WERE, BUT ALSO CREATED THE POSSIBILITY OF INFLUENCING NATURE BY MEANS OF SACRIFICES, PRAYERS AND OFFERINGS. OTHER CREATURES PERFORMED SIMILAR ROLES — FIRE-BREATHING DRAGONS, THE PHOENIX RISING FROM THE ASHES, GIANTS AND MERMAIDS.

LEFT Our dreams are a way of entering the world of myths and legends. By identifying with the characters in our dreams we may learn something about ourselves.

TIMELESS, UNIVERSAL TALES

In preliterate societies, the most common way of passing on these understandings, values and beliefs was in memorable stories that could be told and retold. Their significance was easy to understand, and the characters, creatures and events that were portrayed had a universal relevance. In this way, stories became part of the cultural vocabulary of any society, and the creatures of myth and legend are deeply embedded in our psyche; in our dreams we use them as signposts to the qualities that they embody, as icons.

ENTERING THE WORLD OF MYTH

In our dreams we are free to enter mythical worlds. We can don a mask or join a procession, engage with the king or the fool, the warrior priest or the god of winter. We can even become that character – try out its role, take on its greatness.

These dreams put us in touch with our instinctive and intuitive selves – a side of us that may need attention. They may be an emotive plea from our unconscious mind to dance in the moonlight, to worship the corn, to make a sacrifice or an offering. But we are also fragile beings who are subject to all sorts of fears; myths both allay those fears and add to them.

GODS AND GODDESSES

Mythical figures probably appear in our dreams in much the same way as they did to our ancestors. In our dreams, making an offering to calm a raging god makes sense to us just as it did in real life to our forebears. Our unconscious processes have not changed, although just as our own personal experiences affect how we understand any dream element, our relationship with these figures will be based on how we respond to what they typically represent to us.

We create gods and goddesses so that we can feel safe and protected, so that we can absolve ourselves of responsibility for something; but in their creation we also unleash the terrible aspects of such deities – death and destruction, their capricious nature, their awesome powers. We create them to protect us but we may also come to fear them, and we learn to deal with this dichotomy in dreams of myths. We are shown that the qualities and powers these supernatural beings have in abundance exist within us if we have the courage to acknowledge them.

HYBRID CREATURES

Myths and legends from around the world and through the ages are filled with creatures that are part animal and part human, or that are a mixture of two or three different creatures, and have an element of danger. Mermaids – half fish and half beautiful woman – have been blamed for many a shipwreck, as they lure sailors on to the rocks, while the sphinx, with the head of a woman and the body of a lion, is notorious for strangling travellers who cannot answer her riddles.

Minotaurs, griffins, satyrs and centaurs join the line-up of hybrid creatures from the realm of myth and legend. All have particular associations from the tales in which they feature, but they also embody qualities of the creatures they comprise. In this way, the sphinx may have qualities of femininity but also

the ferocious, uncompromising strength of a lion, and by virtue of her behaviour in the Greek legend could represent any threatening and somewhat enigmatic character, particularly if associated with knowledge and learning, such as a punitive teacher. In a sense, by dreaming of a hybrid creature we are hedging our bets, or efficiently representing several qualities in a single character, trying to resolve anomalies in our lives.

PEOPLE

Not all the characters in myth and legend are fantastical. People appear throughout these tales, sometimes in elevated roles as kings and queens, other times as ordinary mortals who are caught up in greater things. Either way, they could be used to illustrate the ideals and extremes of human nature – heroism, bravery, love, power and so on. Such tales also illustrate some timeless human quandaries and problems, such as the tragedy of Oedipus, who unknowingly kills his father and

marries his mother; the agony of the endless task of Sisyphus, who is obliged to push a rock up a hill, only to have it roll down as he has almost reached the brow. By working with these characters in our dreams, we work with the qualities that they embody and the battles that they fight.

ABOVE The mythical figures in our dreams usually have something very profound to convey. **ABOVE LEFT** Hybrid creatures can remind us of the beast within us all. **ABOVE FAR LEFT** Giant figures may assume the status of gods with the power to create or destroy life.

MYTHICAL DREAM

"In my dream I was walking through a forest. I could hear the birds singing and could feel the warmth of the sun on my skin. A soft breeze was blowing. As I walked, I came to a tiny cottage – it might sound far-fetched but it really did look like a gingerbread house, the kind you read about in fairy-tale stories. The house looked so inviting and I was tired and hot from walking, so I went up to the door and walked inside. I remember walking up a few stairs and going into a bedroom. It wasn't a room I had ever seen before. As I went in, I heard the front door downstairs click shut and the room I was in became shadowy. I started to feel afraid. There was a dark-haired man at the window and he was trying to get into the room. I tried to run away, but my legs wouldn't move. I woke up shouting.

At first it was difficult to revisit this dream or nightmare, but I decided to focus on what the man at the window represented. As I worked with the dream, to my amazement he turned into a golden-haired Apollo kind of figure, a sort of sun-god. I interpreted this to mean that I am afraid of my own power. I see it as something dark or 'bad', so I try to run from it, but actually it radiates light."

ALIENS AND UFOS

WHEN FACED WITH THE UNKNOWN WE OFTEN TRY TO MAKE SENSE OF IT — IN THE FIRST INSTANCE IN TERMS OF WHAT WE ALREADY KNOW WELL, AND THEN PERHAPS IN TERMS OF CONCEPTS FROM THE REALM OF FANTASY OR SPECULATION, OF WHICH WE COULDN'T POSSIBLY HAVE ANY REAL EXPERIENCE. DREAMING OF ALIENS, SPACE SHIPS, FLYING SAUCERS AND SO ON MAY BE OUR WAY OF EXPLAINING AND VISUALIZING THE INEXPLICABLE SITUATIONS OR PHENOMENA THAT WE ARE TRYING TO UNDERSTAND AND COME TO TERMS WITH. WHEN WE HAVE TO FACE THE UNKNOWN WE TRY TO GIVE IT A FACE, A PERSONALITY. THE CREATURES FROM OUTER SPACE SERVE THIS PURPOSE WELL; THEY ARE, BY DEFINITION, ALIEN.

ALIENS

It is surprising how the aliens in our dreams are often very similar. How much this is due to us all watching the same films, and how much it is the manifestation of a new archetype that has developed in our collective unconscious, is difficult to tell. Indeed both could be true, and it is simply that the film-makers are the ones that give shape in a visual way to the archetype.

THE ALIEN WITHIN

Everything in a dream comes from within yourself – you create all of it for your own personal consumption, and there is nothing in it that is actually alien.

If you are creating images of aliens then they represent some part of you that feels alienated or frightened of the unknown – or exhilarated by it. Some part of you is acknowledging an aspect of your life that is manifesting as alien or foreign, that has not been incorporated into your self-image, your lifestyle or your personal environment.

Aliens are often represented as scary, unpredictable creatures that seem bent on threatening our existence and invading our planet. In this way they provide an easy metaphor for situations in our own lives where we feel threatened or invaded by something or someone over

which we have little or no control. It is also significant that we have little understanding of these creatures – we cannot comprehend or anticipate their motives or intentions, and we often have no way of communicating with them. They are unknown and unknowable, and consequently we have no idea of the scale of the threat. Dreaming of aliens is often our way of working through situations that make us feel anxious – perhaps confronting head-on the source of our anxiety and allowing us to try out ways of dealing with it.

Many people feel that they do not fit into society; they feel

BELOW RIGHT Some of the most mysterious phenomena on Earth have been connected with aliens from outer space. **BELOW** When it comes to dreams of aliens and UFOs, there does seem to be some form of universal symbolism that we all understand.

different from most other people they meet, and an encounter with aliens may be a positive, life-affirming experience. Being abducted by aliens may show a yearning for an alternative society where they feel they belong, or it could be an expression of belief in the existence of a society where they are valued.

SPACE TRAVEL

If aliens use UFOs as their vehicle for accessing or invading us, flying saucers, space ships and rockets might well also offer a dramatic avenue of escape for us. It may be that we actually want to break out of our limited world, and such craft offer us a way of literally reaching for the stars, exploring the unknown, having adventures not normally possible in real life. Seeing Earth receding into the distance may help us to stand back and see our world in perspective, in the context of the vastness of space.

ABOVE The concept of UFOs is fascinating. In our dreams they could represent a dramatic way of leaving the everyday world behind.
LEFT To dream the aliens are landing may mean that we should be prepared to encounter something new or strange in our lives.
BELOW When we break out in our dreams we may be trying to break out in our waking life. Spiralling weightless in the galaxy could suggest a spiritual, enlightening experience.

SPACE DREAM

"The sky was full of glowing space ships, full of smoking beings. We were firing guns and bullets at the space ships and the aliens were falling down dead everywhere, bleeping as they died. But there were more of them than I could count and they didn't all die – some were landing. Then I woke up."

This was the dream of a six-year-old child who was worried about starting in a new class at school. In his dream the aliens represented the threatening situation he was having to face and his lack of control over it.

PROPHECY

ABOVE Some people have dreamt about plane crashes and other disasters before they have happened, but prophetic dreams are actually quite rare.
ABOVE RIGHT What looks like a prophetic dream may have a metaphorical meaning: are you living on a knife edge?

WE USUALLY FIND PROPHECY MANIFESTING IN DREAMS IN TWO DIFFERENT WAYS — FIRSTLY AS DREAMS IN WHICH WE FORESEE FUTURE EVENTS (OR FEEL THAT WE DO SO), AND SECONDLY AS DREAMS IN WHICH WE, OR OTHER CHARACTERS IN THE DREAM, ARE TRYING TO LOOK INTO THE FUTURE. WHETHER OR NOT YOU BELIEVE IT IS ACTUALLY POSSIBLE TO SEE INTO THE FUTURE, BOTH THESE KINDS OF DREAMS MIGHT SUGGEST THAT YOU FEEL A NEED TO DO SO; WHETHER IT IS THROUGH INSECURITY OR CURIOSITY IT IS WORTH ANALYSING WHY, OR WHAT IT IS YOU WANT TO FORESEE.

PROPHETIC DREAMS

There have been countless reports of people having a dream that changed their life. They saw an elevator accident, so the next day they took the stairs and the elevator plunged to the ground, killing everybody in it. Or they saw a ship sinking and cancelled their cruise holiday, although hundreds of other passengers perished. Or perhaps they may have dreamt of a car crash and saved their lives by catching the train the next day.

Perhaps we should be a little sceptical of these many urban legends. Only the success stories survive — we do not get to hear of those who took a different course of action than planned and this subsequently turned out to be the wrong thing to do. Nor do we hear of people who change their plans because of a dream and find that it made no significant difference in their lives. Dreams of prophecy are actually very rare. And yet in those cases that actually do turn out to be prophetic we are dealing with something outside of the normal, something mysterious and inexplicable. It's only when we have had a dream that came true ourselves that we can judge whether such a thing is possible. Once it has happened to us we believe, we know, we don't doubt.

It may also be that we dream how we want the future to be, and having already created the desired scenario, we find we are more able to make it happen. In this way the dream may seem prophetic, but it might be more accurate to think of it as a prompt or suggestion.

GAZING INTO THE FUTURE

Wanting to know what the future holds in store seems to be universal — no matter what society or what period in history you look at, you will find seers

---

PROPHECY DREAM

"I'm a keen tarot reader, so I'm not surprised when I find myself doing this in my dreams. In this dream I was with a female friend of mine who is single. She and I were having a glass of wine together, sitting on purple cushions. We started playing with the tarot, and she turned up the card of the Lovers. I remember thinking that I must remember to tell her, that it looked like she would meet someone special very soon.

I actually had forgotten the dream until a couple of months later, when sure enough my friend started a new relationship! Then the memory of the dream came flooding back and I told her what had happened. I think I need more practice in recalling my dreams if they are to be any use!"

and prophets, in addition to numerous tools or methods employed, often by ordinary people, to foretell events that have yet to happen.

In your dream the kind of person who is foretelling the future may be significant – is it one of the great prophets (a biblical figure, perhaps, or Nostradamus) whose predictions may hold the authority of their fame and greatness, or is it a fairground "gypsy" in fancy dress, who gazes into a crystal ball and puts on something of a performance for you, and may just be pulling the wool over your eyes? How credible they are and whether you believe in prediction is critical to how much you believe what you hear.

Some kinds of prediction rely on a kind of sixth sense, while others make use of consistent and well-established methods, such as tarot reading, palmistry, astrology or numerology, and to some extent make their projections on the basis of existing trends or patterns. Either way there may still be a leap of

faith. Much of our desire to see into the future is an expression of our desire for certainty and clarity in a world that is so uncertain and so complex that clarity is hard to find.

We turn to prophecy to help us make decisions we are faced with, or to reassure us that we are on the right path. Dreaming of prophecy could be showing you that you need to make some choices, or clarify what the issues are before you can do so. You may fear something is going to happen, and express your anxiety by trying to find out what you are going to be faced with.

ABOVE Our desire to know what the future has in store is universal. The symbolism of tarot cards can be interpreted in a similar way to dreams.
ABOVE LEFT Whether or not we can see into the future is open to debate. To dream of gazing into a crystal ball may mean you are looking for direction.

LEFT Traditionally, virgin priestesses were attributed with the power of "second sight". If such a figure appears in your dreams pay particular attention to what she is trying to communicate – it could be very important.

MAGIC

IN ESSENCE, MAGIC IS ABOUT TWO THINGS — CHANGE AND POWER. WITH MAGIC, DRAMATIC TRANSFORMATION CAN BE BROUGHT ABOUT IN OUR LIVES, WHETHER WE ARE THE AGENTS OF CHANGE OR WHETHER SOME OTHER MAGICAL FIGURE IS ABLE TO PERFORM HIS OR HER ART ON US. WHOEVER HAS THE ABILITY TO PERFORM MAGIC HOLDS GREAT POWER, ESPECIALLY OVER THOSE ORDINARY MORTALS WHO DO NOT. WITH MAGIC WE CAN DO THINGS THAT WE ARE NOT NORMALLY ABLE TO DO, AND WE FEEL BOTH THE JOY AND THE DANGER OF HAVING THIS IMMENSE POWER. MAGIC CAN ALSO MEAN TRICKERY, HOWEVER, AND IT MIGHT BE THIS CHARACTERISTIC THAT WE ARE DREAMING OF.

ABOVE Animals often take on supernatural characteristics. If you dream of an unearthly creature you need to explore your dream fully to find out what it means. In some cultures a black cat is said to symbolize good luck.

TRANSFORMATION AND CHANGE

Dreams about magic may be a sign that we need to make changes, within ourselves or in our environment. They can be about movement or the lack of it, about being stuck and needing to make effort and expend energy in order to move on, to free ourselves from stagnation and from feeling stuck in a rut. Magic gives us an extra boost to get us to see things differently and get us moving again.

MAGIC AND POWER

In our dreams we can perhaps move objects, conjure up demons, raise a storm or calm a sea. We can kill or heal from a distance, transform people into other creatures with the wave of a wand, and become invisible.

We have probably all wished occasionally that we could do these things in our waking lives. This would give us tremendous power and perhaps it is this that we are after when we dream about magic. Sometimes it would be wonderful to wave a magic wand and make everything better, to change things that are in reality beyond our control — even to subjugate those who normally hold us in their power. We may take great delight for instance, in being able to turn a bullying boss into a tiny mouse, or an unfriendly neighbour into a puff of smoke.

Conversely, having magic performed on us, particularly if it is done against our will, or if it is done by characters who have bad intentions or who in our waking lives have authority over us, can be immensely disempowering and could be drawing our attention to a lack of power or control in our lives. A dream of losing powers that we felt we previously had can also have a similar effect.

HOPES AND FANTASIES

In a more general sense, though, dreaming of magic allows us to work out our fantasies — in our dreams nothing is impossible if we want it to come true, and we have the power to live out our hopes and desires. Dreams also prompt us to look at certain areas of our life that may be lacking in some way, and teach us what we need to do to make things happen. While in a literal way the tricks of magic in our dreams may only be possible in a dream world, their underlying truth can be carried into our daily lives and give us something to work with.

PURVEYORS OF MAGIC

In our dreams it is important to look at the nature and intentions of those who hold the magical powers — whether they are our allies or are threatening and potentially harmful characters is vital to understanding why we are dreaming of magic.

Witches and wizards, as well as magicians and sorcerers, may be sources of good or evil alike. Magicians enthral us with their sleight-of-hand performances, but such trickery may also be more than entertainment, prompting us to look at people in our lives who deceive and trick us, who are trying to pull the wool over our eyes. We need to

LEFT Witches, devils and impish creatures have traditional associations with magic. Check to see if the figures are benign or menacing and what it is they are trying to bring about in your dream.

look at how we might be living a lie, lulled into a false sense of security by our own illusions or those put out by others. In Jungian thought the archetype of the Magician is also known as the Fool, whose surface folly disguises hidden depths of wisdom. Being outside the normal order of society he can say things that no one else would dare to, and thereby shows us things we might otherwise avoid looking at.

THE TRICKS OF THE TRADE

Spells, potions and magic wands are the typical tools of witches and wizards and their presence is another indicator of magic dreams. Being "spellbound" in a dream is akin to being in the thrall of an influential person in waking life, and indeed the lesson to be learnt from such dreams could be to look at whether you are overly impressed by someone, being taken in or manipulated by them, or attracted to something in them which is not real.

If you think the dream character does seem to correspond to someone in your waking life, take note of your gut response to them, notice how trustworthy they are, and try to see beyond any surface appeal.

ABOVE A tall pointy hat and a broomstick are a witch's standard regalia. How often do you find yourself wishing you had the power to make radical changes in your life?

ABOVE The sorcerer's art lies in combining powders and potions to make spells. To dream of sorcery may mean that you need to take an inventive approach to a problem, or perhaps put things together in a unique, but powerful, way.

RIGHT A wizard is a powerful magic maker but make sure he is genuine. Is there someone in your life who has an unhealthy power over you?

THE SUPERNATURAL

THE MYSTERIOUS WORLD OF THE SUPERNATURAL IS INHABITED BY GHOSTLY FIGURES, VAMPIRES, WEREWOLVES AND A HOST OF OTHER CREATURES. MANY OF US LIKE THE COMFORT OF FAMILIARITY, AND FIND THE IDEA OF THE SUPERNATURAL DISTURBING AND TERRIFYING. BY AND LARGE WE AVOID CONTACT WITH THIS WORLD, BUT SOME SEEK IT OUT AND LINK UP WITH IT IN SÉANCES OR BY EXTRA-SENSORY PERCEPTION (ESP). DREAMS OF THE SUPERNATURAL CAN IMPLY THAT OUR PSYCHE WANTS US TO SPEND MORE TIME AND EFFORT INVESTIGATING SUCH MATTERS AS ACKNOWLEDGING OUR SHADOW SELF. ALTERNATIVELY, WE MAY NEED TO MAKE A RADICAL CHANGE OF DIRECTION IN OUR LIVES.

GHOSTS

When ghosts appear in our dreams they can represent unfinished business. Ghosts are the unsettled spirits of the dead who haven't yet found their place in the hereafter, perhaps because they still have some tie to earthly matters. As ghosts are neither fully present nor fully absent, they raise questions about uncertainty and lack of clarity, perhaps about who we are or what we are doing in our lives.

In ghostly figures we are confronted with our own mortality. They give us some sneak preview of the afterlife, without really offering any explanations. Perhaps they offer some hope as well that our existence does not terminate with our death. We can also see them as shadows of ourselves – personifications of our own dark nature, the shadowy side of our selves that we often dare not face.

How the ghosts behave in our dream and how we respond to them is important in discovering what they mean. Some are invisible, others may be shadowy translucent figures. They may be noisy poltergeists or silent figures that only betray their presence by moving things, pointing to our lack of control over our own environment. They may interact with us, but often don't do so directly. You may feel terrified or stressed, or be comforted by their presence. They may be recognizable as strangers, deceased friends or relatives, or famous people. Your relationship to them as such will also affect what they mean in your dream – for instance the ghost may be

BELOW RIGHT Ghosts and phantoms may haunt us in our dreams and this can feel very unnerving. Try to find out what the ghostly visitation is about.
BELOW Strange unearthly figures may appear in our dreams, but these are usually the products of our dreaming psyche.

GHOSTLY DREAM

"I was sitting in a graveyard surrounded by pale, ghoulish figures. I knew they were out to devour me – it was as if I were destined to be a victim, to have my life drawn from me. There was nothing I could do as these ghastly, ghostly shapes crowded around me. But the horror that woke me wasn't them – it was the feeling of my own quiet acquiescence.

When I was thinking about this dream I realized this was exactly how I was behaving in my relationship, allowing my partner to make all the decisions, and it was burying my personality. On going back over the dream in my mind, I knew that I had to return to that graveyard and shout 'No!' and make them retreat, not just sit there and let them eat my soul."

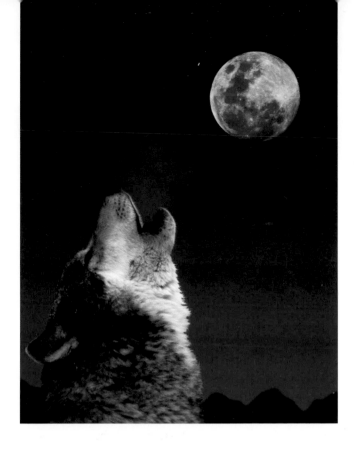

your nagging mother-in-law who is very much alive but casts a shadow over you and is forever interfering with your life.

Ghosts may be all that remain to us of people who have already died, and seeing one may provide a welcome opportunity to have contact with a loved one who has died but whose death you may not yet have come to terms with.

SUPERNATURAL PARASITES

Vampires are the infamous figures of the dead who leave the grave after dark and suck the blood of the living, drawing with it their life-force, or energy, which they need to survive, and often killing their victims in the process. These are the parasites of the supernatural world, and they share this dubious distinction with other ghostly figures such as ghouls, who prey on the dead, and the succubi and incubi, demons who take human form to suck the sexual energy out of sleeping people. In more superstitious times the Catholic Church blamed many a nocturnal

RIGHT A wolf baying at full moon is often associated with supernatural forces. Full moon is when the forces of nature are at their strongest, and traditionally has strong associations with lunacy.

sexual awakening on such apparitions, while in China ghosts are said to be "hungry".

Vampires are defeated by daylight or the simple but powerful icon of the wooden cross, showing us that even such basic forms of protection can give us an escape route from the horror. Indeed, dreams of parasitic ghosts and vampires are often about self-protection. If you dream of these creatures you should look at those aspects of your own life where you feel you are being devoured or having the life sucked out of you. Perhaps you are feeling either used or dominated by your partner, or you have an exploitative boss who makes you work long hours so that you don't have the life or energy to do the things you enjoy. More unusually you may be acting parasitically and have some kind of disturbance around

this. These dreams are our unconscious mind's way of working out such relationships, as well as making us aware that something is wrong.

BATS AND WEREWOLVES

Like vampires, werewolves and bats are nocturnal creatures that suck their victim's blood. A vampire can "shape shift" into a bat, while a werewolf is a human who becomes a vicious beast at full moon. If these creatures appear in your dreams it may be to draw attention to something going on in your life that is frightening or tricky to deal with.

BELOW LEFT Be wary of bewitching figures, as vampires in particular often appear seductive. Who is trying to suck your blood?
BELOW The spirits of the dead come to life at night. A disused building can appear very spooky.

INDEX

ACKNOWLEDGEMENTS

Unless specified, images used in the book belong to Anness Publishing Ltd. With thanks to the following agencies for additional images:

Art Archive: 16l Ragab Papyrus Institute/Dagli Orti; 119tr Musée Carnavalet, Paris/Dagli Orti; 144–5 *Queen of the Night*, Mozarteum, Salzburg/Dagli Orti; 146l *The Wild Swans* by Otto Svend, Dagli Orti; 147t *The Tower of Babel* by Pieter Breughel the Younger, Dagli Orti; 148 *The Depths of the Sea* by Sir Edward Burne Jones, Private Collection; 149c *Mount Helicon with Pegasus and centaur Chiron* by Giovanni Falconetto, Palazzo Arco, Mantua, Italy; 153b *Libuse* by Vitezlav Karl Masek, Musée National d'Art Moderne, Paris/Dagli Orti.

Corbis: 7tl Ron Lowery; 7ct Ryszard Horowitz; 7cb Markku Lahdesmaki; 7bl Benjamin Rondel; 10b Art Becker Photo; 11b Digital Art; 13t Mug Shots; 13c Firefly Productions; 15tl Gianni Dagli Orti; 15 Adam Woolfitt; 15br *Charlemagne Receiving the Monk Alcuino* by Jean Victor Schnetz, Archivo Iconografico; 16r *Portrai of Ibn Rushd* by Andrea di Buonaioto, Archivo Iconografico; 17cl Mug Shots; 20 Michael Boys; 21tl Alfred Ko; 25bc B.S.P.I.; 29t Bill Ross; 32 Julie Meech/Ecoscene; 33cl Ted Spiegel; 36r Galen Rowell; 46–47 Markku Lahdesmaki; 48 Dale O'Dell; 49t Al Francekevich; 49c Layne Kennedy; 50 David Woods; 51l Mendola/Doug Chezem; 51r Rick Gayle; 52tl Edward Holub; 52b Ted Horowitz; 53l Lawrence Manning; 53c Rick Gomez; 55 L. Clarke; 55c Joe Baraban; 56l LWA/Dann Tardif; 56r Paul Hardy; 57bl Jim Erickson; 57bc LWA/Dann Tardif; 57br Randy M. Ury; 58 Mark L. Stephenson; 59tl Markku Lahdesmaki; 59tr Benjamin Rondel; 59c John Heseltine; 59br Elizabeth Opalenik; 60–1 *Fairies Dancing* by Blake, Bettmann; 62l Myron Jay Dorf; 62c Michael Pole; 62r Jon Feingersh; 63tl Bo Zaunders; 63tc Anthony Redpath; 63tr Strauss/Curtis; 63bl Ariel Skelley; 63br Pete Saloutos; 64l Jose Luis Pelaez, Inc.; 64r James Noble; 65t Steve Prezant; 65c Ron Slenzak; 66 Roy Morsch; 67tl Mark Garten; 67tr John Acurso; 67c Terry W. Eggers; 67b Bill Binzen; 68l Norbert Schaefer; 68r Nancy Brown; 69bl Ronnie Kaufman; 69bc Westlight Stock; 69br Jose Luis Pelaez, Inc.; 70l Elena Segatini Bloom; 70c Jon Feingersh; 70r Douglas Kirkland; 71tl Trinette Reed; 71tc Gianfranco Benvenuto; 71tr Patrik Giardino; 71b Cheque; 74 Oddo & Sinibaldi; 75tr Lester Lefkowitz; 75c L. Clarke; 75bl Michael Barley; 75br LWA/Stephen Welstead; 76 LWA/Dann Tardif; 77t Mark Tuschman; 77c 2 Face; 77b David Woods; 80–1; 83tl Joe Bator; 83tr Roy Morsch; 83b C. Moore; 84r Markku Lahdesmaki; 85bl Don Mason; 85br Brian Bailey; 87t Bill Varie; 87c Jose Luis Pelaez, Inc.; 87b Paul Barton; 88 LWA/Dann Tardif; 89tl Alan Schein Photography; 89tr Anthony Redpath; 89c Jose Luis Pelaez, Inc.; 89br Mauro Panci; 90l Roy Morsch; 90r Robert Sememiuk; 91tl Shutter & Mouse; 91tr Tony Arruza; 91b Kevin Muggleton/Tim Bird; 92l Javier Pierini; 93t Steve Starr; 93b Rick Gayle; 94r Joel Sartore; 95 Andrea Pizzi; 96l Arthur Beck; 96r Julie Lemberger; 97l Robbie Jack; 97r Chuck Savage; 98l George Disario; 100 Franco Vogt; 101tr Roy McMahon; 101b Chris Carroll; 102 Chiselvision; 103t Robert Cassel; 103c Sandford/Agliolo; 104–5 Christie's Images; 106l David Chmielewski; 107t Ron Lowery; 107c Steve Chenn; 109c Chuck Savage; 110l Markku Lahdesmaki; 111t Dale O'Dell; 112r Firefly Productions; 113t Jim Cummins; 116r Tim Davis; 117bl Myron Jay Dorf; 118r Philip Wallick; 119b *The Triumph of Death* by Pieter Brueghel the Elder, Archivo Iconografico, S.A.; 121tl Sanford/Agliolo; 121tr Al Francekevich; 121b Rob Lowery; 122l Bob Witkowski; 122r Roy Morsch; 123t Robert Bowen & Ryszard Horowitz; 123b Masahiro Sano; 124 Herrmann/Starke; 125tl Bill Ross; 125tr Markku Lahdesmaki; 125b Grafton Marshall Smith; 126–127 Swim Ink/Griff Teller; 128l Bruno; 128r Ed Bock; 129t Sandford/Agliolo; 129bl Tom & Dee Ann McCarthy; 130t 2 Face; 130b Jeff Vanuga; 131t David H. Wells; 131b David Aubrey; 132l Denis Scott; 132r Firefly Productions; 133tl Roger Ressmeyer; 133tc Jim Erickson; 133tr Third Eye Images; 133b Galen Rowell; 134l Michael Setboun; 134r Philip Harvey; 135l David Raymer; 135r Lester Lefkowitz; 136 Derek Trask; 137tc Mark L. Stephenson; 137br Joe Bator; 138l Cynthia Diane Pringle; 138r Tom Young; 139t Marianne Haas; 139ct T. Kevin Smyth; 139cb Kelly-Mooney Photography; 141t Larry Lee Photography; 141bl John Lund; 141br Dale O'Dell; 142tl Lawrence Manning; 142b Firefly Productions; 143t Ed Bock; 143bl Ronnie Kaufman; 143br Jon Feingersh; 147br Chiselvision; 149l Chris Hellier; 149r Araldo de Luca; 150r Stocktrek; 151t Jim Zuckerman; 151b Dale O'Dell; 152r John Lund; 153tr Paul Barton; 154 Peter Steiner; 155tl KJ Historical; 155c *The Love Potion* by Evelyn De Morgan, Massimo Listri; 155b Strauss/Curtis; 156l Douglas Kirkland; 156r Mark Kessell; 157t Jeff Vanuga; 157bl Gerhard Steiner; 157br J Richardson.

Fine Art Photographic Library: 59bl *A Bright and Happy Christmas*, Anon; 147bl *The Lily Fairy* by Falero.